THE WORLD UPSIDE DOWN

By the same author:

Les commentaires du Tao tö king jusqu'au VIIe siècle (Paris: Collège de France, Institut des Hautes Études Chinoises, 1977).

La révélation du Shangqing dans l'histoire du taoïsme (Paris: École Française d'Extrême-Orient, 1984).

Taoist Meditation: The Mao-shan Tradition of Great Purity (Albany: State University of New York Press, 1993.

Introduction à l'alchimie intérieure taoïste: De l'unité et de la multiplicité. Avec une traduction commentée des Versets de l'éveil à la Vérité (Paris: Les Éditions du Cerf, 1995).

Lao zi et le Tao (Paris: Bayard Éditions, 1996).

Taoism: Growth of a Religion (Stanford: Stanford University Press, 1997).

Isabelle Robinet

The World Upside Down

Essays on Taoist Internal Alchemy

Edited and translated by

Fabrizio Pregadio

Golden Elixir Press

Golden Elixir Press, Mountain View, CA
www.goldenelixir.com

ISBN 978-0-984308262 (pbk)

Typeset in Sabon.

Cover: The *xuanpin* (Mysterious-Female), a Taoist symbol that represents
the unity of Yin and Yang. The two trigrams are Fire (Yang, above) and
Water (Yin, below), which respectively enclose True Yin and True Yang,
represented by their inner lines.

Contents

Acknowledgements

"The World Upside Down in Taoist Internal Alchemy" was originally published as "Le monde à l'envers dans l'alchimie intérieure taoïste" in *Revue de l'Histoire des Religions* 209 (1992): 239–57. English translation published with the permission of the Collège de France.

"The Alchemical Language, or the Effort to Say the Contradictory" was originally published as "Mystique et rationalité: Le langage dans l'alchimie intérieure taoïste ou l'effort pour dire le contradictoire" in *Asiatische Studien / Études asiatiques* 47 (1993): 645–62. English translation published with the permission of the Schweizerische Asiengesellschaft.

"Role and Meaning of Numbers in Taoist Cosmology and Alchemy" was originally published as "Le rôle et le sens des nombres dans la cosmologie et l'alchimie taoïstes" in *Extrême-Orient — Extrême-Occident* 16 (1994): 93–120. English translation published with the permission of the Presses Universitaires de Vincennes.

"On the Meaning of the Terms *Waidan* and *Neidan*" was originally published as "Sur le sens des termes *waidan* et *neidan*" in *Taoist Resources* 3.1 (1991): 3–40. English translation published with the permission of the Society for the Study of Chinese Religions.

The World Upside Down
in Taoist Internal Alchemy

INTRODUCTION

Internal alchemy, or Neidan, is a technique of enlightenment whose earliest extant written records date from the eighth century. It appeals both to rationality, which gives order to the world, and to what transcends rationality: the unspeakable, the Totality. Its main tools are the trigrams of the *Yijing* (Book of Changes) and a number of key metaphors, some of which are alchemical in nature, whence the name, "internal alchemy."

Alchemy begins with a binary structure made of two complementary and antagonistic terms: pure Yin and pure Yang. However, their binary structure admits complexity with two other mixed terms, born from the union of the first two: Yin containing Yang, and Yang containing Yin. A neutral term, the Center, is beyond the conjunction and the disjunction of the other two.

The principle consists in ordering the world by means of multiple and complex reference points built on the basis of these initial data and of a multi-layered structure. Here lies the rationality of alchemy, in the sense of providing order and intelligibility. However, being a didactic technique oriented toward mysticism, alchemy also involves the denial of its own system. This denial is achieved by several means: the reminder that silence is the foundation of the word; the continuous evocation of Unity, which merges and abolishes all reference points; the adoption of a fundamentally metaphoric language that must be surpassed; the recurrent disruptions in the continuity of discourse; the use of images that play at several levels, operating now in one direction, now in the opposite, levels that are related to one another until being unified; the ellipsis that handles two different

1

entities as equivalent; the reciprocal encasing of all images, so that "the child generates its mother" and the contained is the container; the multiplicity of facets, times, and reference points superimposed above one another, which counteracts the fragmentation wrought by rational analysis.

The alchemists, therefore, use a highly structured language, but transgress it by introducing a negation of their own system, and by expressing, through a system of reciprocal encasing, a duality absorbed into Unity, a rationality traversed by irrationality. The language of alchemy is a language that attempts to say the contradictory.

One facet of this system is the theme of the "world upside down."

> Look at the gate of death as the gate of life,
> Do not take the gate of life to be the gate of death.
> The one who knows the mechanism of death and sees the reversal
> Begins to understand that the good is born within the evil.[1]

> The Sun in the West, the Moon in the East. Heaven is Earth, Earth is Heaven. This symbolizes the growth and union of Yin and Yang, the reversal [of the course] of the five agents.[2]

"Reversal" (*diandao*) is one of the basic principles of internal alchemy. This principle takes many forms and is applied in different ways. To obtain the Golden Elixir—the equivalent of the Philosopher's Stone—one should go through several reversals. According to a sentence often quoted in the texts, "Those who go in the ordinary sense give birth to human beings; those who go backward find immortality."

Li Daochun (fl. ca. 1290) explains that there are two directions. One of them follows the ordinary course and goes toward the end: it is the "operation" (*yong*), the actuation. The other goes backward, and consists in returning to the Origin: it is the "substance" or the "body" (*ti*) of all things.

> If you know the origin and ignore the end, you cannot expand; if you know the end and ignore the origin, you cannot attain the foundation of subtlety. Those who go back to the Origin are vaguely and indistinctly joined with the Ultimateless; those who

---

[1] *Wuzhen pian*, "Jueju," poem no. 62.
[2] *Ziyang zhenren wuzhen pian zhushu*, 8.13b.

2

go to the end are born, transform themselves, and die endlessly. Going backward and going forward are necessary to one another, because the origin and the end are not two.[3]

However, the ordinary persons who "follow the course" generate other beings. The seekers of immortality, who go backward, generate an embryo of immortality within themselves: they self-regenerate.

The ordinary course follows the sequence of the seasons—winter, spring, summer, and autumn—and the sequence of four of the five agents associated with the seasons: Water, Wood, Fire, and Metal (see tables 1 and 2). The alchemists often insist that the opposite course causes Water to generate Metal, and Wood to generate Fire. Since Metal is related to the West and its traditional emblem is the Tiger, they say that the Tiger emerges from Water and the North. Similarly, Wood is related to the Dragon and the East, but emerges from Fire and the South. Therefore the backward rotation is performed by going from North to West, and from South to East. Time is traced in a backward sequence. The normal flow of time leads to death; those who seek immortality move toward youth and birth.

> The wheel of Heaven turns to the left; the Sun, the Moon, and the planets turn to the right. The wheel of Heaven turning to the left causes the movement of the four seasons; the Sun and the Moon turning to the right transform the ten thousand beings.
>
> Therefore red cinnabar, which symbolizes Fire, is placed in the South, and is the Red Bird. As it moves to the East, this cinnabar generates Mercury, which is of a green color and symbolizes Wood; it is placed in the East and is the Green Dragon. Black lead belongs to Water, is placed in the North, and is the Dark Warrior. As it turns to the West, black lead generates White Silver.
>
> Therefore it is said that Fire turns to the East and is the Dragon (while Fire traditionally is the Red Bird and turns to the West), and Water turns to the West and is the Tiger (instead of being the Dark Warrior).
>
> This means that the True Breath of the Great Tripod secretly moves according to the turning of Heaven; and as for the symbolism of the Moon, the Sun and the planets, they turn to the right.

---

[3] *Quanzhen jixuan biyao*, 9b-10a.

But within the Tripod there is only the One Breath, and not external objects.[4]

Thus, Fire going East and Water going West turn toward the left, contrary to the traditional sense.

YIN AND YANG

One of the basic principles of Chinese internal alchemy consists in using two elements that by themselves summarize the entire alchemical Work. The two principles are Yin and Yang, but can be symbolized by West and East, Metal and Wood, Dragon and Tiger, Fire and Water, the feminine and the masculine, and so forth. However, an important feature of this discipline is that it is only concerned with True Yin, which is the Yin enclosed within Yang, and with True Yang, which is the Yang enclosed within Yin. These are the concealed core, the hidden internal truth; they are the materials or the "ingredients" of alchemy. The goal here is to bring the internal and the hidden toward the external and the visible.

In terms of trigrams, the picture can be described as follows (see tables 6 and 7). Two trigrams are at the origin of all others, their father and mother. They are Qian ☰, which is related to Heaven and is made of three Yang solid lines, symbolizing pure Yang; and Kun ☷, which is related to the Earth and is made of three broken lines, symbolizing pure Yin. Qian and Kun joined and gave birth to the other trigrams, two of which are especially important for the alchemist: Kan ☵ and Li ☲. The inner line of Kan (a Yang line enclosed between two Yin lines) and the inner line of Li (a Yin line enclosed within two Yang lines) are True Yang and True Yin, respectively. Their multiple meanings and functions cannot be fully described here. Let it suffice to say that they represent the trace and the union of the father and the mother; and that they express above all a fundamental principle of interdependence: there is no Yin without Yang, and vice versa, or there would be sterility.

One text says:

> Reversal does not consist in thinking that the Yin is Yang, but in taking the Yang from the Yin. It does not consist in thinking that

---

[4] *Jindan fu*, 24a-b.

the Yang is Yin, but in taking the Yin from the Yang. When the Yin is the Yin and the Yang is the Yang, this the forward course, the ordinary way of the world. Taking the Yin within the Yang and the Yang within the Yin is the mechanism [of life] stolen by the immortals.[5]

Since alchemy is concerned in the first place with the inner lines of the trigrams Li and Kan, the paradox of reversal consists in considering Li as female, while logically it should be male because its Yang-masculine lines are predominant. Analogously, Kan should be female, but is considered to be male. "The Sun is Li and belongs to Yang, and instead it is a girl. The Moon is Kan and belongs to Yin, and instead it is a boy. This is the reversal."[6] But there is also the reversal of the reversal; the Yin within Li is Fire (Yang), and the Yang within Kan is Water (Yin).

ABOVE AND BELOW, FLOATING AND SINKING

Since the inner lines of Kan ☵ and Li ☲ are the traces of the opposite elements born from the union of the primary trigrams, namely Qian ☰ and Kun ☷, they are regarded as having the same dynamic characteristics as Qian and Kun—in other words, of Yang and Yin, respectively. Yang tends to rise, and Yin to descend. Therefore Kan, which is in the North (Yin) and is placed below in the traditional arrangement of the Chinese compass (see table 7), tends to rise under the influence of its inner Yang line. Li, in contrast, tends to descend. Here we see a reversal not only of movements, but also of customary hierarchies: the boy is below, the girl is above.[7] In an analogous way, and paradoxically, fire descends and water rises, because Li is fire, and Kan is water.

In order to set all of this into motion, one should extract the Metal found within the Water. This reverses the traditional order of generation: Water now generates Metal. Thus Metal moves contrary to the customary way and rises to the left. Going in the opposite direction, it rises to the North, placed at the bottom of the compass, and then moves to the West. It is said to "emerge" or to "float," contrary to the earthly laws that cause metal to sink into the water. And even though

---

[5] *Ziyang zhenren wuzhen pian zhushu*, 4.7a.
[6] *Xiuzhen shishu*, 26.27a.
[7] *Ziyang zhenren wuzhen pian zhushu*, 2.12a.

it is outside, Metal is called the host, while the guest, contrary to the ordinary laws, is the Yin found within man.[8]

The Yin rising under the action of Yang is also compared to water that is placed below and rises, while fire is above and descends. This is contrary not only to the natural laws, but also to what happened during the formation of the world, when Yang rose to Heaven and Yin descended to the Earth. The movement, in other words, is the reverse of the one that once gave and continues to give birth to the world. Xue Daoguang (?–1191) formulates this as follows:

> Li is Fire, fire burns and goes upward; the nature of Fire and Wood is to float, and they are Yang. Therefore they are said to be the hosts. Kan is Water, water flows and goes downward; the nature of Water and Metal is to sink. Therefore they are said to be the guests (the host is placed above, according to the ordinary rites). This is the ordinary way. But if Li, instead, is considered to be female and Kan is considered to be male, then the host becomes the guest, and the guest becomes the host.[9]

This world turned upside down is represented by several images:

> In the operation of the backward movement of the Saint, [the order of] Kan and Li is reversed, and we say that Fire is above and Water is below. On the cosmic plane (lit., the plane of Qian and Kun), Earth is above and Heaven is below. In terms of sexual relations, the man is below and the woman is above.[10]

Physiologically, the same thing happens. In sexual intercourse, according to the ordinary way, essence—which is Yin and liquid—descends down to the testes along the spine, but "in alchemy it is not so: we follow the reverse route; when man is in complete quietude, both physical and mental, the Yang arrives within the body to the kidneys, and causes the Lead prior to the world to move. Lead rises to the head (the upper Cinnabar Field), then descends to the heart (the Purple Palace), and returns to the Yellow Court (the center of the body), where it transforms itself into the Elixir."[11]

---

[8] See, for example, *Ziyang zhenren wuzhen pian zhushu*, 2.10b-11a.
[9] *Ziyang zhenren wuzhen pian sanzhu*, 1.12a-b.
[10] *Ziyang zhenren wuzhen pian zhushu*, 2.12a.
[11] *Ziyang zhenren wuzhen pian sanzhu*, 3.24b-25a, with a few omissions.

The physiological aspect is only one among others in an alchemy that plays on several levels. "Dragon and Tiger are not the liver and the lungs (as they are in the classical breathing exercises): they are the True Yin and the True Yang in the heart and the kidneys."[12] In a very concise statement, another text says: "The lower part of the body sends forth the Fire, the upper part of the body sends forth the Water."[13] And again:

> With regard to floating and sinking, Fire rises and Wood floats (they are Yang), they are above and are the hosts (i.e., they are in the place of honor). Water descends and Metal sinks, they are below and are the guests. This is the way of men and the law of the world, the ordinary course of the five agents. However, although Fire and Wood tend to rise, they are caused to descend and become the guests, and although Metal and Water sink, they are caused to rise and become the hosts. This is the way of the immortals.[14]

Another text says:

> The art of the reversal of the five agents is the Dragon coming forth from Fire. The five agents do not follow the ordinary course, and the Tiger is born from Water. The Yang Dragon fundamentally comes forth from the trigram Li; the Yin Tiger, in turn, is born from the trigram Kan.[15]

Reversal is also a repeated extraction (*solve*) of the inner core:

> The kidneys are Water. Within Water a Breath (of a Yang nature) is generated that we call True Fire. This Fire obscurely contains the Water of the True One, which we call Yin Tiger. The heart is Fire. Within Fire a liquid is generated that we call True Water. This Water obscurely contains the Breath of True Yang, which we call Yang Dragon.[16]

Thus, from the Kidneys (Water) one draws the Breath (True Fire), from which one draws the Tiger (True Water); and from the Heart

---

[12] *Dadan zhizhi*, 1.8a.
[13] *Chongyang zhenren jinguan yusuo jue*, 9b.
[14] *Ziyang zhenren wuzhen pian zhushu*, 2.12a.
[15] *Dadan zhizhi*, 1.8b.
[16] *Id.*, 1.8a.

(Fire) one draws the True Water, from which one draws the Dragon (Breath of True Yang).

Li Daochun explains:

> In terms of trigrams, Dui ☱ (located in the West in the arrangement "posterior to the world") is Metal. The nature of Metal is to sink. From Metal, Water is born, which corresponds to the North and to number 1, and is Kan ☵. Within Kan, True Fire (its Yang line) rises, and therefore it floats. The trigram Zhen ☳ is Wood. The nature of Wood is to float. The lower line of Zhen is full (Yang), and from Wood, Fire is born, which corresponds to the South and to number 2, and is Li ☲. Within Li, True Water (the inner line of Li) descends, and therefore it sinks.[17]

Then the author continues the same argument in terms of Metal and Mercury, the alchemical ingredients. Metal rises by means of Fire, and Mercury sinks under the influence of Water. Similarly, at the level of "symbols" (*xiang*), the Moon, which pertains to Kan (North, Water), should in the first place descend, but now rises under the action of fire. The Sun, which pertains to Li, should rise, but withdraws and sinks. Therefore the Dragon, which usually is an aquatic animal and in alchemy symbolizes Wood and the East, emerges from Fire, which in the "ordinary" rotation should emerge from Wood; and the Tiger, which pertains to Metal and the West, emerges from Water, while it is the Tiger that normally should produce Water.[18]

According to the "generative" sequence of the five agents, Water generates Wood, which generates Fire, which generates Soil, which generates Metal, which generates Water (see table 3). In the backward movement, just as the Tiger emerges from Water, so does Water generate Metal, and Fire generate Wood. This inversion is commonly expressed by the sentence "the child generates its mother,"[19] which concisely expresses the pair of contrary movements, "forward" and "backward." Metal generates the Water that generates Metal. This is also the movement of the recursive loop, the endless rotation in which beginning and end meet one another.

If we look at the trigrams in the arrangement "prior to the world" (see table 7), we see that—apart from Li and Kan, whose role

---

[17] *Qing'an Yingchan zi yulu*, 1.11a.

[18] See, for example, *Zhouyi cantong qi fenzhang tong zhenyi*, 2.22a.

[19] See, for example, *Ziyang zhenren wuzhen pian zhushu*, 4.7a.

in the alchemical Work is different—the Yang rises by going to the left, and the Yin grows by descending in the same direction. Therefore if one goes backward in the contrary direction, on the right side of the circle from North to West and then to South, Yin decreases. Since the human being is considered to be Yin, and the adept seeks to purify his Yin and to become pure Yang, if he goes "backward"—that is to say, toward the right—he returns from winter to summer through autumn. In this way he reduces his Yin and reaches the South-summer, which is pure Yang.

THE MOON

The Moon plays an important symbolic role in the context of "reversal." As we have said, the Moon is Yang in alchemy, contrary to what it is usually considered to be: "Heaven holds the Sun, which is Yin, or Yang containing Yin; the Earth holds the Moon, which is Yang, or Yin containing Yang."[20] For us, earthly human beings, the Moon therefore is Yang, again by virtue of the principle that the internal—here the Yang—prevails over the external.

At the same time, this does not prevent an alchemist from retaining the normal order as well, and from considering the Moon to be also Yin:

> The Moon is the Great Yin. Fundamentally it is provided with matter, but is devoid of light. It waxes and wanes depending on whether it receives more or less light of the Sun. . . . In the early morning of the first day of the month, the Moon separates from the Sun; then it receives the light of the Sun and becomes luminous. . . . According to the way of speaking of the alchemists, Metal fundamentally is born from the Sun. In the early morning of the first day of the month it receives the influence of the Sun (just like the Moon); it is the True Metal or Great Yin that is born from the Palace of Kun (Water, pure Yin), and that fundamentally is transformed by the true Fire of Great Yang. When it begins to receive its light, it is like the Moon that receives the light of the Sun.[21]

[20] *Id.*, 7.18a.
[21] *Zhouyi cantong qi fahui*, 3.13a-b.

Each day without Moon or of new Moon, the Great Yin and the Great Yang join in the same palace. The Moon then is black and has no light. During the second and the third stages, the trigram Li and the Sun gradually recede and the Sun sends forth its light; the Moon arises and becomes luminous. Its small *hun* soul (the Yang soul) gradually increases, while its *po* soul (the Yin soul) gradually decreases.[22]

The author continues by describing the path of the waxing and waning of the Moon, and ends with a sentence often repeated by the alchemists: "It goes around and begins again, revolving like an endless ring. This is the transformative movement of the celestial Dao, and it occurs naturally."

One should begin the alchemical Work when the Moon emerges, the instant in which Yin grows and the reflection of the Sun appears in the South-West, which is also the gate of the "return" of the Sun (see table 5). This location is designated by the calendrical marker *geng*, which serves here as a spatiotemporal marker, and by the first trigram that contains a Yin line.[23] It is the location where, after the conjunction of the Moon and the Sun—a symbol of the primal undifferentiated state—the Moon "leaves" the Sun, and a Yin line appears in the trigram that corresponds to this instant. It is "the cavity of the Moon," in honor of which the masters have written poems, "the opening in the world" through which the adept will be able to "participate in the wonder of creation before its beginning".[24]

When a Yin line and the Moon, reflecting the Sun, appear, one should begin the Work and collect the rising Yang by "incising Chaos," which is similar to a closed flask and is raw matter. In the arrangement of the trigrams according to the state "posterior to the world," this time corresponds to the place of Kun, pure Yin, the original Mother. The Moon therefore is the symbol of the human being who is Yin and contains a Yang line. The adept follows its journey; but in order to "heat" Metal and purify it, he must capture the Yang line within the Yin. This is symbolized by the Moon, which traditionally is said to contain a rabbit that represents the Yang line.

---

[22] *Huangdi yinfu jing jiasong jiezhu*, 2.6a.
[23] See, for example, *Ziyang zhenren wuzhen pian zhushu*, 6.7b-8a; and *Zhouyi cantong qi fahui*, 5.8b.
[24] *Shangyang zi jindan dayao*, 4.2a and 5.13a.

ENCASING

The principle of reversal can take several meanings. It is obviously related to the themes of androgyny and of the hierogamic exchange of attributes. It is also the image of the corporalization of the spirit and the spiritualization of the body. Reversal also consists in considering the internal—which is closed in an envelope that is contrary to it in nature: the Yin within the Yang, the Yang within the Yin—as the "true nature" of the ingredients manipulated in the alchemical Work. This procedure is dynamic, because the Yang tends to rise and the Yin to descend.

Another meaning is that of encasing and extraction. A fundamental principle of alchemy is to "cut," that is, to separate and extract in order to purify (this corresponds to the *solve* of the Western alchemists). The image of the jewel in its ore is often used in this context. The principle of reciprocal encasing provides a double face and a reverse side to each of the elements in question. One extracts the Metal that is in the Water, and again the Water that is in the Metal. These indefinite encasings and extractions represent the fundamental principle according to which, as the alchemists like to repeat, there is no Yang without Yin and vice versa; otherwise, they add, there would be infertility. The system appears to be binary, but actually it is quaternary, or even quinary if one counts Soil, which acts as a catalyst or a "matchmaker," as the authors say. One author states: "True nature (*xing*, classified as Yang) comes from the vital force (*ming*, which is Yin), and this vital force returns to the true nature."[25] In other words, one draws the *xing* from the *ming*, which must return to the *xing*. Here the reversal of encasings forms a recursive loop.

COINCIDENCE OF OPPOSITES

As shown by one of the sentences quoted at the beginning of this essay, a third meaning of "inversion" is the coincidence of opposites. Chinese alchemy expresses this principle in many other ways; first of all, as we saw above with Li Daochun, by using two inverse rotations at once. Here is an application: Metal generates Water, and descends from the West to the North. There, *under the action of Fire*, it is

[25] *Jindan zhizhi*, 3b.

purified and rises; then it reverses its movement and goes again toward the West ("the child generates its mother"). In this way, one reconciles the two opposite rotatory movements, the leftward one and the rightward one.

This means that one uses, concurrently and transparently, two ways of arranging the trigrams, the one "prior to the world" and the one "posterior to the world." In the arrangement "posterior to the world," the trigram Kan ☵ (Yin containing Yang) is in the North, below, and corresponds to Water. In the arrangement "prior to the world," it corresponds to Metal and is located in the West. Thus Kan is North and Water according to one system, West and Metal according to another. At the same time, the alchemists place the trigram Li ☲ above and the trigram Kan below, which corresponds to the arrangement "posterior to the world"; but they enjoin the practitioner to advance according to the arrangement "prior to the world," i.e., in the direction of the Yang growing in the leftward direction.

Thus the two ways of arranging the trigrams overlap one another. The alchemist depicts both the human level ("posterior to the world") and the celestial level ("prior to the world"). By doing so, Kan ☵ and Kun ☷ (pure Yin, found below in the "prior" arrangement), the two trigrams located in the North under either scheme, are deliberately confused. In addition, the very nature of the elements obtained is contradictory. Chen Zhixu (1290–ca. 1368) says:

> The one Yin line within Li is feminine, and the one Yang line within Kan is masculine. The Yin within Li is Fire (this reverses the reversal, as Fire is known to be Yang), the Yang within Kan is Water. . . . The Yin within Li is Mercury and is the Essence (of a Yin nature); the Yang within Kan is Lead and is Breath (of a Yang nature).[26]

There are therefore a female Fire and a male Water, or an "aqueous fire" and an "igneous water," as a Western alchemist would say.

The author of a commentary on the *Wuzhen pian* (Awakening to Reality) wrote about this coincidence of opposites:

> Metal can overcome Wood, and Wood can overcome Soil (this is the rule in the ordinary course of the agents). These three natures are made of different matter; they swallow one another and de-

vour one another, and yet we can bring them to approach one another. This is the method of "reversal."[27]

A further example among many others is given by Li Daochun:

> Kan ☵ fundamentally is the substance of Kun ☷ (pure Yin), therefore it is called Great Yin. . . . Li ☲ fundamentally is the substance of Qian ☰ (pure Yang), therefore it is called Great Yang.[28]

These designations should logically be reserved for Kun and Qian, respectively. We can see that there is a symbiosis between Kan and Li, the mixed elements, on the one hand, and Qian and Kun, the pure elements, on the other. In both pairs of trigrams, the first one designates the North, and the second designates the South. This is the case in both ways of arranging the trigrams—"prior" and "posterior to Heaven," which are again superimposed on one another.

We see this again in the parallel and almost symbiotic relation that exists between two diametrically opposite points, the South-East and the North-West, that mark the beginning of the Work. Thus, the time of "gathering" is often called *zhen geng*, two words that respectively designate a trigram and a spatiotemporal marker, one of which is located in the South-East and the other in the North-West. This is because the Moon, which rises in the South-West (the gate of the "return" of the Sun at the winter solstice), is related, as we have seen, to the North-East, the gate of the exit of the Sun at the winter solstice.

The *materia prima* of the alchemists must be gathered when the Moon emerges in the South-West, and this *materia* is found in the North-East. These two points, says one author, are "the beginning and the end of the routes of Yin and Yang."[29] The place of exit of one is the place of return of the other. The South-West, called the "cavity of the Moon," is the "gate of men," but is also called the "gate of the Sun." The North-East, where one should "gather" the *materia prima*, the first ray of Yang prior to the world, is the "gate of the Moon," but also the "gate of the ghosts": it is the gate of the growth of Yang. One of the two points, therefore, is the gate of the

---

[27] *Ziyang zhenren wuzhen pian jiangyi*, 6.7b.
[28] *Zhonghe ji*, 3.26a.
[29] *Zhouyi cantong qi fenzhang tong zhenyi*, 2.2b.

growth of Yin, and the other is the gate of the growth of Yang. According to Chen Zhixu: "On the third day of the month, in the location of [the spatiotemporal marker] *geng* (i.e, the South-West), the Yang of the North (lit., *gui Yang, gui* being the marker of the North-East) begins to emerge."[30] A commentary to the *Wuzhen pian* says:

> The Moon is born from Kun ䷁ (complete Yin), and is obscure. It forms Tai ䷊ (the hexagram corresponding to the spring equinox, which represents Heaven below and the Earth above—the world upside down), and this is its phase of growth. Then it forms the hexagram Jiji ䷾ (Water above, Fire below, the normal order for the heating). When the Moon begins to disappear, from Kun (pure Yin), after the full Moon, it forms the hexagram Pi ䷋ (reestablishment: Heaven above, Earth below), and this is its phase of decrease. Then it forms the hexagram Weiji ䷿ (Fire above, Water below, the opposite of the order for the heating).[31]

Thus, initially, the world is upside down, but fire and water are in the proper positions for the heating of the ingredients. After the full Moon, which marks the end of the first phase, the order is reversed, while the world is made straight again. In the day without Moon, the phase of "yangization" of the Work begins, and in the day of full Moon, "yinization" begins. Here we have again the same short circuit from the full Moon to its decay, from the day without Moon to its growth.

CONCLUSION

The reversal concerns the perspective of departure. At first there is the appearance, the immediate intuition of the visible things, the self-identity of beings: pure Yin and pure Yang (Qian and Kun), each placed at one of the two poles. Then a shift occurs that reverses the first intuitive, "naive" apprehension, and deconstructs the principle of self-identity: the object is no more identical to itself ("pure"), but contains its opposite (Li and Kan at the two poles); and since this contrary element enclosed within counts as its true identity, the object is identified by its contrary. Something similar to a change in algebraic

---

[30] *Shangyang zi jindan dayao*, 6.5a.
[31] *Ziyang zhenren wuzhen pian zhushu*, 7.16a.

sign occurs, and the values are reversed: the Yang principle is represented by a young girl, the Yin principle by a young boy.

This change in algebraic sign (positive-negative) presides over a deconstruction that prepares a reconstruction (the Elixir, immortality). With a displacement of identities, things are dislodged from their immediate definition, from their identity to themselves, in favor of a displacement to the other, its opposite, through a structure of multiple and multidimensional perspectives. This raises the issue of meaning, which is established through exchange operations and reciprocal interactions that are determined by the formal articulations needed for any distribution system. Returning to oneself from the other, returning to the world after leaving it: Water generates Metal that generates Water.

Moreover, the alchemists tie both approaches to one another. The Yang values are represented by a series of concepts, symbols, and images that are traditionally placed on the Yang side: summer, the trigram Qian, the *hun* soul (i.e., the Yang soul), and the heart, which is related to fire; among them, however, they also place the *ming* (vital force), which the same author has explicitly ranged on the Yin side. The same applies to items classified as Yin.[32] When the authors express themselves more concisely, they resort to formulations that are utterly paradoxical and contradictory: the Dragon (Yang) is both the *xing* (true nature, Yang) and the kidneys (Yin). Furthermore, by superimposing the pattern "prior to the world," that of the noumenon, to the pattern "posterior to the world," that of the phenomena, they state in their own way the same truth as the Buddhists, when they say that *saṃsāra* is *nirvāṇa*, and vice versa.

From the perspective of immortality, to which the Taoists adhere, they reverse space and time and make both of them circular and reversible: the flow of things is nothing but the process of continuous cosmic emanation. The Taoists reverse this flow in a double-sided process: they reverse the "negative" values of life, seen as a loss of energy, a dissolution, a dispersal, and give them the positive value of a continuous emanation that creates the world, where beginning and end meet.

However, as we have seen, Yin contains the True Yang, which in turn contains the Yin. In a cycle of endless encasings, even reversal is performed in reverse.

---

[32] See, for example, *Chongyang zhenren jinguan yusuo jue*, 17a-b.

The Alchemical Language,
or the Effort to Say the Contradictory

INTRODUCTION

The alchemical masters face the universal problem of transmitting and translating the unspeakable into words. "How can we seek the mysterious and the wondrous in a discourse?" asks Zhang Boduan.[1] The Dao is unspeakable and the mystical experience is inexpressible; yet, say the masters, in order to expound and transmit them, one is bound to use the language. Mindful of the words of Zhuangzi, according to whom one could speak for a whole day without saying anything, but also be speechless for a whole day without ever being silent,[2] they resort to a language that leaves space to silence, which they always evoke, to the unspoken, and to the additional meanings. Since there is always something left unexpressed, the masters summarize and remind what has already been said, they repeat and expand the old discourses, attempting at the same time to recover the world, the language, and the use that was done of it, and to complete and renew it.

The alchemists' undertaking, nevertheless, consists in methodically relying on language in order to transmit and to instruct. Reminding the value of silence is not sufficient: they try to introduce it in their discourse. They reiterate that their discourse is only a vehicle that leads to the wondrous, or—using another image of the *Zhuangzi*—a

---

[1] *Wuzhen pian*, "Jueju," poem no. 2.
[2] *Zhuangzi*, chapter 27; trans. Watson, *The Complete Works of Chuang Tzu*, p. 304: "With words that are no-words, you may speak all your life long and you will never have said anything. Or you may go through your whole life without speaking them, in which case you will never have stopped speaking."

net that must be discarded once the prey has been captured.[3] They intend to "give form to the Formless by the word, and thus manifest the authentic and absolute Dao," says Li Daochun (fl. ca. 1290), who adds that words are only steps to be climbed, and that once the highest point has been reached, no word applies anymore.[4] "There is a mechanism that surpasses them. This is not easy to explain, but one should comprehend beyond words."[5]

Chen Zhixu (1290–ca. 1368) makes a distinction between "the way that establishes a discourse," which consists not only of words but also of practices, fasts, meditations, etc., and the "transmission of the heart," a concept borrowed from Buddhism. This transmission tightly combines action and non-action, and is the "Great Way" of alchemy. Chen Zhixu explains that the intent of Taoism is to convey the "wonder" of true emptiness, the fullness intertwined within emptiness —unlike Buddhism, whose mission is to show that "wondrous emptiness is not empty." In other words, the task of the Taoists is to insist on the positive aspects of emptiness. They emphasize, to a larger extent compared to the Buddhists, the reality of the world, which is made even more real by being traversed by emptiness. This is why, adds Chen Zhixu, one should give materiality to that reality by the intermediation of language.[6]

Peng Xiao (?–955) designates the cosmic Man, founder of the world, as the Saint. Accordingly, he states that "he has not lightly created a discourse that would mislead the future generations. Therefore he has called the Sun and the Moon as his witnesses, has examined the luminous spirits, has separated the firm (Yang) from the flexible (Yin), has shown and revealed Metal and Water, has taken the Dragon and the Tiger as metaphors, and has used images (xiang)."[7] For the alchemical masters, however, saying is not enough. They want to show. They must actively urge their disciples to walk along the

---

[3] *Zhuangzi*, chapter 26; trans. Watson, *The Complete Works of Chuang Tzu*, p. 302: "The fish trap exists because of the fish; once you've gotten the fish, you can forget the trap. The rabbit snare exists because of the rabbit; once you've gotten the rabbit, you can forget the snare. Words exist because of meaning; once you've gotten the meaning, you can forget the words. Where can I find a man who has forgotten words so I can have a word with him?"

[4] *Zhonghe ji*, 3.13a-b.

[5] *Id.*, 3.22b.

[6] *Shangyang zi jindan dayao*, 8.3b-4a.

[7] *Zhouyi cantong qi fenzhang tong zhenyi*, 1.6b.

same path and find out by themselves. Li Daochun says: "I would like to show you directly [the meaning of my discourse], but I am afraid that you will not believe me and will not be able to put it into operation (*yong*). You must know by yourselves."[8]

In fact, the alchemical masters deliberately use metaphors that they invite to surpass:

> The way of alchemy entirely consists of metaphors (*xiang*). It takes Lead and Mercury as substances, but one must know that the "essence of Lead" and the "marrow of Mercury" are nothing but metaphors. It is based on the terms Li and Kan, but one must know that the "Kan boy" and the "Li girl" are nothing but empty terms. It uses the forms of the Dragon and the Tiger, but one must know that the "Dragon-Fire" and the "Tiger-Water" have no form. It talks about the "yellow sprout," the "divine water," and the "flowery pond," but these are things that can neither be seen nor used.[9]

Just like one should go beyond the phenomenal appearance of things, so it is necessary to surpass the letter of the texts and of their codes, pondering at the same time the inexhaustible meaning that they contain. When the alchemists say that all of their language consists only of metaphors, this means that they disguise the Truth, that they do not speak it because this is something that cannot be done. It also means that what they speak about differs from the meaning of the words that they use, because this is, paradoxically, the most correct way of conveying what is impossible to say. Their language functions by means of a distantiation that is continuously reminded: the finger is not the moon, the net is not the prey. Only the allusive mode that they systematically use can account for the double character of existence—which is and at the same time is not, which acquires fullness by being traversed by Emptiness but cannot be apprehended in itself, and of which one can only grasp the appearance and the trace.

The alchemists, therefore, create their own language. Somehow it must function—they *must* make it function—in front of the adept in order to say what has already been said many times, and could be summarized in a few words. Paradoxically, the speaker is not the

[8] *Zhonghe ji*, 3.3b.
[9] Xiao Yanzhi, mid-thirteenth century, in *Xiuzhen shishu*, 9.12b.

master himself. On the one hand it is the Dao: like the Saint, one should "establish the teaching by embodying Heaven, and transform the people through the action of the Dao."[10] But, on the other hand, it also the Neidan, the method, the pedagogic artifice—that is, the language. Witness to this are the many quotations and the constantly repeated *leitmotivs* that embroider the texts: their redundancy is intentional. And since this language is symbolic and possesses multiple facets that are revealed by making them turn around and around under different lights, the masters are not weary of letting this language mirror itself, of playing its multiple layers, of discovering in it relations and enunciations that are always new. Their language, in fact, is also the fruit of a reflection on language; and it aims to stimulate the continuation of that reflection.

The word "mirror" leads us to consider another aspect of this manipulation. The alchemical language is a mirror play, an immense enigma that embeds many smaller ones, a *koan* similar to those of Zen. Neidan indeed acts on the adept as a *koan*, as a conundrum whose efficacy resides precisely in the sort of seduction and fascination that it clearly instigates on those who use it—be they the masters or the adepts. It is a mechanism that they are never tired of playing: chants, poems, essays, dialogues, and charts are produced by the masters and are requested by the disciples, are unceasingly transmitted, augmented, broken up, and then recomposed. The numerous commentaries on the major Neidan texts are examples of these decipherings that could vary without end. The masters display in them their creativity; the adepts find in them something on which they can fix their spirit, and make it operate. But, as the texts say, it is in emptiness that the figures of this language, the *xiang*, are suspended, all fastened to one another.

Yet, the masters entrust these figures, the *xiang*, with the task of operating on the spirit of their disciples. In a way, this alchemy forms an immense synecdoche. The entire Yin-Yang binary system on which it operates is the sail that is blown by the boat, but at the same time makes the boat move. This discourse by means of figures serves to indicate that the discourse *in its entirety* consists only of figures. And this rhetoric of provisional figures aiming to their resolution is on its own a figure of speech, and signals a speech on the figures.

---

[10] *Zhonghe ji*, 3.4a.

The conception that the masters have of the operational mode of language is intimately related to the conception that the Chinese tradition has of it; under this light, it is probably not by chance that Taoism—the religion that, unlike Buddhism, has the deepest roots in China—has followed this way. As is well known, the Chinese have little inclination for theoretical and abstract thought, independent of factual situations. Abstract names are absent from their language, and the conditional is hardly used in it.[11] Neidan shares the same active conception of language with Confucianism, even though it maintains that language cannot really convey the entirety of meaning.

Made of a constant intertextuality and a constant production of meaning, the texts labor and are themselves a labor, a practice. They can be perpetually reinvented starting from a paradigm that is never exhausted, from a founding Text that is not written but is readable, which is the Dao, or the Truth, and from the method of interpretation, the alchemy. Each user of a text is inevitably called to be one of its creators: here lies the very function of a text. He is invited to find new forms for it, in a ludic way. This paradigmatic text is therefore a collective work, whose origins cannot be located and whose individual particularizations—through its reading, its performance, its writing, or its system of expressed or implicit references— are single instances that open themselves up onto all others. Each text and each commentary is an example of productive and creative reading in an infinite play of mirrors that reflect one another as far as the eyes can see, even though each of them is oriented in a slightly different way so that the aggregate, which is never finished and is always plural, opens itself up onto the entire universe, which is never closed or never finished. In this sense, the texts do not let themselves be measured. Thus the true reader is the one who perceives the infinite plurality of the text, which is an image of the plurality of the universe, of its multivalence that admits its own reversibility and its own con-tradictions; and the one who perceives the non-canonicity of the "canonical" texts like, for example, the *Wuzhen pian* (Awakening to Reality). This means that these texts are "classical," canonical, and foundational because they do not have only *one* real sense, and are created precisely in order to contain simultaneous multiple senses.

---

[11] Hall and Ames, *Thinking Through Confucius*, pp. 269 and 272.

In addition to being a medium of communication, language is also a means of ordering the world and of giving it a meaning. Through language, a possible world can be articulated and a desired world can be structured; through language, that project can be communicated and the creation of that world can take place. According to the Confucians, as Léon Vandermeersch has aptly remarked, the prince owns the word: he names, and by doing so, he "gives order." The founding heroes of Chinese civilization, Yu the Great or Fu Xi, who drew the world in order to organize it, are witnesses of this. The "names" are the tools by which the sage organizes the world—this is an axiom that enjoys a large consensus among Chinese thinkers. This conception has led them to reflect on the good use of language. For them, language affects the behavior, and the effect verifies the sense and the truth of a term or a discourse.[12] Within Confucianism, for which the social tissue is a fundamental reality, the name of an individual and even his title correspond to a personal and ontological reality. They are not merely signals, but testimonies of intelligibility: the problem of language is related to the axiological status of beings and entities. The same conception of the active force of language and of names is also found within the Shangqing tradition of Taoism, where knowing the names of divine places and divine beings is indispensable for salvation. This conception of language allows one to consider that language may be re-generating, that the subject can be re-created by means of the language. This is context in which the alchemy takes place.

This typically Chinese conception of language is supplemented by the alchemical masters with a concern—no less typically Chinese—for *determining* the position of concepts and images in relation to one another; in other words, for marking the distances that exist between the individual concepts and images and the paths that lead from one to the other, as well as the directions taken by those paths. The alchemists express this with insistence, saying that it is essential to know the laws that govern the reciprocal relations and proportions of Yin to Yang and vice versa, as well as their movements of increase and decrease. Therefore the way in which Yin and Yang evolve is what they are. The meaning of the terms lies in the description made of their operations. This pertains to an "operational" concept of meaning.

[12] Hall and Ames, *id.*, p. 263.

The alchemical masters would probably agree with Wittgenstein when he says that thinking does not lie in associating representations with words, but in "operating with symbols."[13] Thus there is for them an equivalence between an element, its position, and its movement. We find, for instance, a commentator who explains the word "to float" with the term "Mercury," adding: "Mercury is above, and it is said to float."[14] And another one who says: "A moment is a place. A place is a thing."[15]

However, for one who intends to testify to transcendence, or simply to testify how the world moves, language is also an obstacle, a screen that can hardly disclose the underlying truth, which is too rich and too large. On the one hand, the conception that the Chinese have of language gives more power to the discourse, but on the other hand, it makes it more opaque. In order to break through this thickness one must break it by multiplying the names. A preface to the *Wuzhen pian* says: "Sometimes we construct a metaphor with a single thing, but apply it in entirely different ways; sometimes we make images with different things, but the referent is one."[16] Many words or images for a single reality: the sense is not entirely in the word or the image. Many realities for a single term: the sense is not fully attained in the referent. One should fight against the always menacing underside of realism.

Even beyond that, the alchemist does not fight only against the words' opacity and authority. Their discourse is made by means of figures, but the meaning is devoid of figure (*wuxiang*). The truth that one should try to say or think goes, by its own nature, beyond the saying and the thinking. There is a constant danger of reifying it, while it should be maintained alive, multiple, and mobile. Therefore one should fight against the human spirit; or rather, one should work, and cause the others to work, on the human spirit, in order not to halt at the words, which are provisional intersection points among complex relations. The result is that one of the functions of the alchemical language is to destabilize those who stick to their habits of thought, to the terms or the schemes. For the masters, the point is not simply saying the truth, but teaching how to think the truth. The discourse of Neidan is not deemed to be the discourse of a subject, but the dis-

[13] Wittgenstein, quoted by Bouveresse, *Le Mythe de l'intériorité*, p. 310.
[14] *Cui gong ruyao jing zhujie*, 13a.
[15] Yu Yan, *Zhouyi cantong qi fahui*, 2.21a.
[16] *Ziyang zhenren wuzhen pian zhushu*, preface, 3b.

course of life. It is a discourse with an objective intent, where the enunciating subject is either erased, or multiple.

"Nobody understands me," laments the author of the *Wuzhen pian*, evoking the sighs uttered in the *Daode jing* (Book of the Way and its Virtue).[17] This means: I do not aim for compliance; I do not say anything of what people expect; my language is not conditioned by the recipient of my words. I speak the true, not the plausible or the admissible.

An enigma in itself, suited to the enigma of life, Neidan proposes one enigma after the other and invites one to penetrate and solve them. It engages and keeps awake, and incites to exercise. One must walk through the different associative meshes that it fashions, organize them and reassemble them, make connections among them and then undo them. One must interpret and translate. Much more than by giving explanations, the masters instruct by showing how the action should be performed, how one should practice. Instead of providing definitions and interpretations of the signs that they employ, they demonstrate their usage. The "explanations" that are given do not explain anything; they do not intend to say the reason of the rule, but to illustrate the application, and to give an operative description.

We have an example of this way of operating with the reply given by Li Daochun to a disciple who asks "how can there be water in fire, and fire in water." Li Daochun replies by illustrating the mechanism that plays on different registers: the natural laws, the alchemical images, and Taoist physiology. On the plane of the natural laws, he says that "Water cannot moisten by itself; it must be heated by Fire and be transformed into vapor. . . . On the plane of the alchemical images, Fire rules in the south and Water receives its breath. . . . On the physiological level, it is the [liquid] moist that is found within breath." In a similar way, but conversely, he says: "There is Fire in Water, like the Sun that emerges from the sea; Water rules in the North, the point where Fire receives its germ of life; it is the breath

---

[17] *Wuzhen pian*, "Lüshi," poem no. 11. *Daode jing*, 70: "My words are very easy to understand and very easy to practice; but in the world no one is able to understand them, and no one is able to practice them. . . . It is only because they have no understanding that they do not understand me; but since those who understand me are few, I am honored."

that is found within the humid essences of the body."[18] This reply merely establishes connections between different registers of images or of language. Clearly it does not attempt to describe meaning as something lying outside language: it explains by means of other words. The proposition "there is Water in Fire" refers to the meaning of a general configuration, of a tabulation that must be understood without being interpreted: it is constantly translated into different perspectives or with different colors; it is animated by other tabulations in order to be understandable; but at the same time, it must be understood immediately and without any additional interpretation. The truth of the tabulation lies in what we understand of it, in its being mobile, and in the comprehension that it induces: a comprehension that is an act, sets in motion, and creates.

In the language of the alchemists, this is accomplished by the *yi*, the creative idea (*idée créatrice*), or the *shen*, or *xin*, the intuitive spirit (*esprit intuitif*), a central catalyzer without which nothing could be done, and which utilizes the signs and relates them to one another (the alchemists refer to it as the "go-between"). It should be attended to, it cannot be interpreted, and is a psychological—rather than logical—term. This "intention" is nowhere; it is "without image" and is immediate, say the alchemists. It is not an entity, and is not even a process: they say that it is here and there, but is outside time. It is neither an activity of spirit nor a state of consciousness. It does not introduce itself between sign and reality, but into an interstitial void "where there is no space." The sense of the discourse is not produced by the discourse: it is direct and immediate.

But the motive of the discourse lies in the training, the apprenticeship and the formation; it lies in the development of an intuitive function that seizes the senses. This discourse is not founded, but founds. It is a discourse "in process,"[19] in a state of actualization, which one follows in its movement; it is a path to be walked. It does not try to persuade at all, and it addresses itself only to those who seek. As it was with the "men possessing recipes" (*fangshi*, the early ancestors of the alchemists), this language exhibits and transmits a "know-how." In other words, it says: "If you want to achieve this

[18] *Zhonghe ji*, 3.27a-b.
[19] Greimas, *Du sens*, vol. 2: *Essais sémiotiques*, p. 176.

result (the acquisition of sainthood), you must perform the exercises that I tell you."

It is a second, artificial language compared to the usual one; a language that, unlike the ordinary languages, does not circulate among people who share it, but between one person, the master, who wants to teach to another one person, the adept. It is a new language that consists in a new way of dealing with thought.

IMAGES

In addition to being productive of meaning, the discourse of Neidan is also figurative. It is a demonstration, a performance. One of its favorite instruments is the *xiang*, and it defines itself as unfolding in the domain of the *xiang*.

The notion of *xiang*, a term that can be translated as "figure," "symbol," "image," has a long history in China, on which I cannot dwell here and for which I shall refer to works that examine it more at length.[20] I will limit myself to give a few indications and to report essentially what the alchemists say about it.

The *xiang* is the Image, which in some respects takes in China, it seems to me, the place that the Word or the sound take in other traditions, such as Tantrism. It does so, however, not as a creating force, which is the role of "Breath" in China; but rather as the form, the configuration (which on the auditive plane is the sound) that comes closest to the original form of beings. The Dao is the Great Image. Images and numbers are provided with a cosmic and cosmogonic efficacy and truth that are close to those of the mantra, but on a mode that is visual rather than auditive.

By defining itself as relevant to domain of the images, alchemy ties itself to the tradition of the *Yijing* (Book of Changes) and to the effort of rationalization and organization of the world represented by the entire art of divination.[21] At the same time, alchemy dissociates itself from Buddhism, which operates without images, as the masters say; this means that the images are an integral part of its operational mode, in opposition to Buddhism (especially Chan), which intends to provide a teaching without words, without mediation. The images are

[20] See Jullien, *Procès ou création*; and Billeter, *L'art chinois de l'écriture*.
[21] See Vandermeersch, *Wangdao ou la Voie royale*.

the mediators of the alchemical teaching. This is clarified by Yu Yan, who substantially says: emptiness means seeing in darkness and hearing in silence, and is not the quietude of Chan; if it were the same, why should we resort to the trigrams and to the symbolism of Yin and Yang?[22]

The term *xiang* ordinarily designates the trigrams and hexagrams of the *Yijing*, whose fundamental language is made of images. The whole Chinese tradition connects the *xiang* to the notion—equally foundational—of numbers. Some authors give priority to the numbers, and others to the images; but they all agree in considering them as complementary to one another. For Zheng Xuan, in the second century, the *xiang* in divination is the primordial aspect (*ti*) of the divinatory chart.[23] More specifically, the images are the symbolic explications of the trigrams that are included in the *Yijing* in the form of commentaries, and that resort to metaphors pertaining to the natural order: heaven, earth, lightning, thunder, winds, mountains, and waters.

For the "Great Appendix" (*Xici*) to the *Yijing*, which is the first text to outline a theory of the images, the images are in heaven the counterparts of the forms on the earth. According to the commentator Han Po (fourth century), this means that the *xiang* are the celestial bodies, counterparts of the earthly configurations such as mountains and rivers. "Heaven has suspended the images," says the "Great Appendix," "in order to show what is auspicious and inauspicious, and the saintly sage has imagined them," meaning both that he has made them into images, and that he has represented those celestial images (the term *xiang* is taken here as a synonym of one of its homonyms that means "to represent," "to make an icon"). What is visible, says the commentary, is called *xiang*, and what has a form is called *qi*, a term that literally means "instrument" and, in this context, is generally translated as "material entity." According to the same text, the material entities belong to the order of "form" in opposition to the transcendent Dao, which is the "Great Image," the "Image without image" (for Laozi and Zhuangzi, "Great" means what includes its own contrary).

---

[22] *Zhouyi cantong qi fahui*, 5.6b.
[23] Vandermeersch, *Wangdao ou la Voie royale*, p. 293.

Isabelle Robinet

Visible, but lying outside the material world, the images place themselves midway between the formless Principle and the material entities. The hexagrams have arisen from the contemplation of those images by the Sage. The notions of auspicious and inauspicious, of firm and yielding, which are cardinal in the *Yijing*, are themselves images that designate success and failure in the first case, day and night in the second one. They are produced by the contemplation, accomplished by the Sage, of the things of heaven and earth, of their movements, interactions, and conjugations, and of the rules that govern them. The formulation of the knowledge of the saintly Sage by means of images is part of his ordering activity, of his "know-how." At the same time, these *xiang* pertain to the celestial order and are formless in relation to the things of the earth. The language that relies on them partakes, therefore, of an ordering activity that regulates itself on the activity of Heaven or of Nature (the Chinese word used here is *tian*, that has both meanings).

"He established the images in order to express his thought, which cannot be entirely expressed in words." This sentence of the "Great Appendix" is the object of a well-known discussion by Wang Bi (226–49). Wang Bi insists on the role of the "image" as a link between the thought and the word. The word should lead to the image that elicits it, and the image in turn should lead to the thought that is contained in it, and to which it gives presence (*cun*). But in addition, like the other members of the "school of the Mystery" (Xuanxue) to which he belonged, Wang Bi underlines the inadequacy of both the word and the image, and the necessity to "forget" them in order to attain to the idea. A famous sentence of his *General Introduction to the Book of Changes* (*Zhouyi lüeli*) is often quoted by the alchemists, who take it as a rule: "When one has attained to the image, one forgets the word . . . When one has attained to the thought, one forgets the image . . . When one has caught the hare, one forgets the trap . . . When one has caught the fish, one forgets the net." Even if the image partakes of the ontological truth of the things of the cosmos, it remains a simulacrum. Its truth lies only in its ability to reproduce: an image can only show. Therefore one must go beyond it.

While the "Great Image" cannot be figured, as Laozi says, the images are "the beginning of movement and immobility," says Li

28

Daochun.[24] He continues: "What can be figured (*xiang*) is the Mother of names and forms." By this he means that the images are at the origin of the world, because "it was by relying on the images that the first sovereigns were able to give order to things."[25] Yu Yan says:

> Yin and Yang within ourselves do not have a form that we can find . . . . Without resorting to images and relying on things, how could we shed light on them so that the others may probe the depths of their Spirit and know its transformations? . . . This is why we deal with this through metaphors, and do not speak.[26]

The images make it possible to rationalize and govern the world. For the alchemists, they are the juncture between the unspeakable of intuition, the inexpressible vision of totality, and the deficiency of discourse—a juncture that one should abandon, like the boat of Zhuangzi, once the shore is attained.[27] They are intermediaries between the plane of the principles (*li*) and the plane of the practice (*xing*). According to Li Daochun, in fact, the plane of the images is situated between the plane of the natural or celestial principles (*li* and *tian*) and the plane of the spirit (*xin*) that pertains to one's behavior, the implementation or actuation of the Dao (*xing dao*). For him, the plane of the images is the one of the Saint who gives order, and pertains to "comprehension" (*ming*).

The images are used as themes that can tie different levels of meaning to one another, both vertically (in depth) and horizontally (in width). They are organized into mobile configurations that can replace one another. Each image is capable of assuming different functions and variations of meaning. The images can constitute a composite configuration, a pattern, or a figurative path, a role, a process. They enable one to put into action certain entities that are tied and refer to one another, and charge these entities with the different levels of existence and meaning that they represent.

[24] *Zhonghe ji*, 1.6b.
[25] *Id.*, 3.5b.
[26] *Zhouyi cantong qi fahui*, 1.11a-b.
[27] *Zhuangzi*, chapter 14; trans. Watson, *The Complete Works of Chuang Tzu*, p. 159: "Nothing is as good as a boat for crossing water . . . . But though a boat will get you over water, if you try to push it across land, you may push till your dying day and hardly move it any distance at all."

One image can have different registers of meaning, and one element can be represented by several images. Thus, the images make it possible to decompose a term into multiple semantic elements. Being related to one another, and being arranged into sequences that refer to one another, the images constitute chains of meanings that unfold endlessly. By taking the terms not as particulars, but as relational and functional, and by looking at them from the point of view of their position in a pattern, one makes them interchangeable. In this way, one creates a tool of contemplation and integration, which involves at the same time the instances and the acting forces, the structure of the action and the basic pattern on which action unfolds.

For example, the images of the Dragon and the Tiger, which are fundamental in Neidan, designate Lead and Mercury; and vice versa, those of Lead and Mercury designate the Dragon and the Tiger. These two pairs refer to one another; neither is more "real" or more fundamental than the other. This equivalence, established by the texts, means that we are dealing neither with the animals tiger and dragon, nor with the heraldic animals of the East and the West that pertain to the Chinese tradition. At the same time, we cannot exclude those emblems, because they convey meaning. And if it is said that Dragon and Tiger are not liver and lungs (the sense they have in the physiological practices), this means that one should not stop at that level; but even that level should not be excluded. By doing so, Dragon and Tiger take on a distinctive meaning, in which the traditional meanings are not excluded, but are integrated and included into a comprehensive configuration that includes "Dragon-Tiger," "Lead-Mercury," "liver-lungs," as well as the trigrams Li ☲ and Kan ☵, and that designates the Yin within the Yang and the Yang within the Yin. This pair also indicates that the intent of Neidan is not to deal, as is usual, with Yin and Yang or with the "young Yin" and the "young Yang," but with their respective substances—namely, the respective contrary elements. The intent of all this is to deal with the process of the conjunction of the opposites.

The Dragon-Tiger couple, says Li Daochun, is only another name of the Yin-Yang couple, which by itself summarizes the entire alchemy:

> The image of the Dragon-Tiger undergoes a thousand transformations and ten thousand changes, and its transcendence (*liao*) is divine and unfathomable. This is why we use it to represent the

ingredients, we establish it as Tripod and Furnace, and we move it with the Fire regime. By analogy, it is Kan and Li; by substitution (*jia*), it is Metal and Fire; by naming, it is the boy and the girl; by conjoining, it is the husband and the wife. All these different names constitute the wondrous function (*yong*) of the Dragon and the Tiger. By virtue of their divine animation (*ling gan*), we call them ingredients; because they bring things to achievement, we call them Tripod and Furnace; by virtue of their transformations, we call them Fire regime; because they cross each other and join to one another, we call them Kan and Li; because they are firm and straight, we call them Metal and Wood; because they ascend and descend, we call them boy and girl; because they wondrously harmonize with one another, we call them husband and wife.[28]

Here is another example of the equivocal use of symbols: Water is a word that designates the Yin, and therefore can designate either the Yin containing the Yang, or the Yin contained within the Yang. But these two "waters" pertain to different levels: one extracts the Yang found within the Yin (which is Water), and from this Yang one extracts the Yin contained in it (which is also Water).

As can be seen in certain translations of Chinese alchemical texts that, for the sake of ease of access, omit all images that pertain to this language, or reduce them to a psycho-physiological or an ethical level, these "figures" are multiple, rich, complex, and pertain to different orders. They confer the speech of a master a tone, a mildness, and a dimension of incomparable greatness and splendor that pertains to them and is part of the fascination that this enigmatic language must have evoked in the spirits of the adepts. It is one of the stimulating elements that attract the disciples, urging them to spend time in this language, to savor it and to ponder on it. Yu Yan, inspired by the "Great Appendix" of the *Yijing*, writes:

> The people of old times who practiced alchemy "looked above and contemplated the signs of Heaven (i.e., the asterisms), looked below and examined the veinings of the Earth (i.e., the mountains and the rivers), and within inspected the heart of man." . . . Heaven and Earth, despite their greatness; creation, however wondrous it may be; the asterisms that distribute light; the five agents and the eight trigrams that arrange themselves in a circle—all of this

---

[28] *Zhonghe ji*, 4.17b-18a.

concentrates in our bodies and becomes our Tripod and our Furnace, our ingredients, our Fire regime. By going backward within ourselves, the Three Powers (Heaven, Earth, and Man) are complete in us.[29]

If one relies on the markers of time to establish the Fire regime, it is only "for fear that one loses the mechanism of the union of Man and Heaven."[30] In other words, the images also serve to provide a cosmic dimension to the alchemical work.

PROCEDURES AND FORMS

The long enumerations of correlations and equivalences that are often found in the alchemical literature, and of the tables and charts that are very much liked by the alchemical authors, serve not only to make things visible and to provide inspiration. Their intent is also to decode, to encourage one to go past what they represent in order to reorganize them into different wholes. While the essentials of Neidan can be summarized in a few sentences—something that the masters frequently do—nothing said in their sentences concerns its actual unfolding, which is an essential dimension of Neidan. The required operations can structurally be reduced to just a few, but can take innumerable and inexhaustible forms. And this unfolding is always presented in a scattered and dismembered form, which asks to be recomposed and restructured.

The discourse of the alchemists bears on the logical discourse, as it relies on conceptual and linguistic categories to which the authors adhere, and to a basic pattern that forms the foundation of their thought and their texts. The discourse, however, is never linear and is often poetical. Its development is never continuous: disruptions of thought and language are applied constantly, and consciously. While the discourse is descriptive, it deliberately moves from one to another plane of perspective, leaps from one to another state of the Work, from the part to the whole, and vice versa. Sometimes it compresses a subject into a few words, sometimes it lingers on a precise point or moment of the Work, and then suddenly and almost prematurely

---

[29] *Zhouyi cantong qi fahui*, 2.13a.
[30] *Id.*, 2.12a.

emerges onto a vision of accomplishment. Or it breaks off on a remark about the difficulty or the simplicity of the Work, or maybe to warn readers against their personal understanding. And the discourse is not only dismembered and fragmented; it is also repetitive. It proceeds by continuous resumptions, it is always the same and always new. Different and multiple images are used to say the same thing, providing different clarifications and forcing the spirit to recover the implicit analogies: one type of logic and its inverse convey the same truth. The discourse does not have the form of a narrative, because time is actually never involved if by this we mean the "before" and "after" of the human time. Just like the actants are only one, so everything happens in the eternity of an instant, and in the eternity of a time that never stops to unfold. The action can be condensed in a few words; but words will never exhaust it and will never account for it, whatever their sequence may be.

The absence of a logical or narrative sequence is such that a fundamental work like the *Wuzhen pian* admits several versions in which the sequence of the poems differs. None of these versions appears, from a logical or a narrative point of view, to be better than the other ones.

Constant interruptions cause shifts from one to another time, from one to another space, from one to another plane of reference— or from the contained to the container, from one temporal dimension to another temporal dimension, from a movement of expansion to a movement of contraction. These interruptions serve to place multiple dimensions one within the others, to impose changes of perspective, to avoid that readers stop at one referent, and to oblige them to constantly encase different spaces and times one within the others. Whenever a substitution is performed between two terms that pertain to different systems of reference—for example, the mineral and the human orders—a change of perspective occurs, but the previous plane is not removed. In this way the multiplicity of facets is constantly preserved in order to attenuate the defects of the inevitable fragmentation of the discourse, and to remove the boundaries that distinguish the different distinctions that are made, for example, among the year, the month, the day, and the hour; or between the human and the cosmic planes; or between the physiological and the mental dimensions.

The reader, thus, is obliged to move continuously from one to another plane or dimension. This should result in identifying those planes with one another, in superimposing them one above the other, and in a comprehension that is based on the relation of equivalence that exists between two or among four terms. Therefore the reader is constantly reminded of the identities that occur among the terms of the discourse, the phases and the stages of the Work, its different subjects and different orientations, and the metaphoric language and the didactic discourse.

THE FUNCTIONING OF IMAGES

I will now to give a concrete example of how the images (*xiang*) constitute a constellation that is related to all other images and attracts them onto itself, while at the same time it unfolds into different directions and makes them converge onto it. I will use as an example the different names given to what the alchemists call the "Tripod" and the "Furnace," which are deemed to represent the frame of the alchemical Work, the site of the alchemical transformations: the ingredients are heated within the Tripod, which is placed in the Furnace.

In order to explain the Tripod and the Furnace, Chen Zhixu begins by saying that they are called in different ways, and that the help of a master is needed to understand the various denominations. Then he lists several names, some of which are cited below:[31]

Tripod of Qian and Kun. Qian ☰ and Kun ☷ are the trigrams of pure Yin and pure Yang. They represent Heaven and Earth, the primal couple, and the "father and mother" of all other couples. They are outside the world, and have at the same time a cosmic and an extra-cosmic dimension.

Walls of Kan and Li. Kan ☵ and Li ☲ are the ingredients, the objects of the operations of the alchemist. This name evokes the functions of a frame and an enclosure. Thus Qian and Kun, or the Furnace and the Tripod, are at the same time the limits of the world, and what ensures its stability and security.

---

[31] *Shangyang zi jindan dayao*, 5.6a.

One Opening of the Mysterious Barrier. This name emphasizes a function of opening, of breakthrough, which is mysterious and unique.

Divine Furnace of the Supreme One. A place of purification, which is divine and pertains to the supreme One, the ancient astral god who animates the world.

Yellow House, Spirit Chamber. This again evokes the enclosure, which is divine and is yellow, the color of the center.

Tripod of the Elixir of Original Chaos. The original unity.

Yang Furnace and Yin Tripod. Two complementary appellations, sometimes opposed to one another, but here taken as synonyms. Are they two? Are they one and the same thing? The alchemists answer that they are at the same time one and two—the Yin-Yang couple— but, like that couple, are interchangeable with one another and refer to one another.

Jade Furnace and Golden Tripod. The Yin-Yang couple is now joined by the couple made by gold and jade.

Furnace of the Reclined Moon. According to the texts, this name is based on the form of the Furnace. It is compared to the waxing Moon, and as such it represents the growing Yang, i.e., the Yin Furnace (the Moon is Yin) that contains Yang. It is "reclined" because it looks on high, meaning that it indicates a growing, arising movement. The symbol is the same as Kan, and thus differs from the other symbols mentioned above according to which the Furnace and the Tripod are tied to the trigrams Qian and Kun. This figure does not indicate anymore the "frame" of the Work, which is fixed, but its progress, whose phases are related to the phases of the Moon. The Furnace here is an indicator of what it contains, which is sometimes denoted by the periphrasis "what is within the furnace shaped as a reclined moon."

Tripod of the Suspended Womb. This is the Yang tripod and designates the embryo of immortality, "because it is not attached to the ground, like a tripod within the hearth." It evokes the result of the alchemical Work.

Furnace of the Two Eights. This term alludes to the two measures of eight ounces of each ingredient. Sixteen ounces form one pound. It means that equal parts of each ingredient are required to form the embryo of immortality, a symbol of totality, because each of the two ingredients, Yin and Yang, is one half of the world. Moreover, there is an allusion to the age of sixteen years, when the Yang breath has not yet weakened and therefore is a symbol of unaltered vitality.

Upper and Lower Furnace. This appellation has a meaning similar to the previous one. The Furnace is constituted by the two halves of the world, above and below, that encase and complete one another.

Internal and External Tripod. Here the two parts suggest the work of interiorization that the adept must accomplish. What is "external" is assimilated to transcendence. In the first part of the Work, called the "external practice" (active and "warrior-like"), the adept should distinguish the two elements and extract them in order to purify them. The second part consists in interiorization; it occurs spontaneously, without conscious intention. It is the slow heating, when the adept "nourishes" and "hatches" the embryo.

If we look again at the names listed above, we can point out several traits of the pair Furnace-Tripod. This pair forms the fixed frame of the Work, the two extreme boundaries within which the Work is to be achieved. But the pair Furnace-Tripod also stands for the center. It refers to pure Yang and pure Yin, Qian and Kun, but also to the trigrams Li and Kan, impure Yang and Yin, each of which contains an element of the other. Thus the Furnace and the Tripod are both the frame and the instruments of the Work.

The pair is double: at the same time Yin and Yang, Furnace and Tripod, above and below, external and internal. But the pair is also One, the supreme One, the Center, the original Chaos. It is a closed framework, but also an opening: opened toward what is above, suspended above the earth.

What we have seen above is an example of how the alchemists manage to summarize the Work in a single figure with multiple facets. Simply by means of the names given to this dual tool, which is deemed to be the container, the content is also evoked—and with it the ingredients, their natures, doses, heating, and phases of heating. Everything is concentrated in what appears to be only one element of the Work; but this element refers to all other elements. Each appellation selects and therefore actualizes one of the facets or one of the actants of the Work and virtualizes the others; and the multiplicity of possible appellations emphasizes the provisional character of the actualized form and its ties to the other forms. In sum, we could not even really consider that Furnace and Tripod are elements of the Work. They are also its locus, and even its loci (frame and center), and are defined by what occurs in them. The texts of course say, for example, that the Center is nowhere: it is characterized by the fact of being the locus of the union, and is an indicator of the other elements because it contains them. But the same can be said of the other elements, because the Work is summed up in the Two, and these Two are summed up in the One.

The images refer to one another and go from one register to the other. Any replacement is possible. The Tripod-Furnace is a multivocal image that holds the possibility of unfolding all the mesh of significations of the alchemical language. We have seen how the multiplicity is reduced to the One, and how the parts are reduced to the Whole by means of an image. We shall now look at some rhetorical artifices used for the same purpose.

RHETORICAL ARTIFICES

The alchemists often use denial as a means of expression. For example, they say: "Everything [in the alchemical Work] is in the body and the spirit, and one should not separate oneself from them; but in fact it is not a matter of body or spirit." Or again: "The time factor is not time, but is not outside time because, without time, one could not begin the Work."[32] But in addition to this simple procedure, they also use more subtle ones. The irrational or, more in general, the place of the unspeakable is expressed by what I will call a "transgression": transgression of the laws of logic, of the laws of language, and especially of the ordinary human laws. The alchemists have a clear consciousness of the transgressive character of their intent, and frequently express it: they emphasize that they go "against the current" and "invert" (*diandao*) the order of things.

Transgression of the human laws, at the very least because the alchemists go "against the current": this is the precise translation of the term *ni*, which they use in this context. We shall return on this subject, but first we must look at certain procedures of transgression in the discourse that are directly related to the law of "inversion."

The alchemists use metonymy in a such way that the ambiguity can be solved only in its own context. It is only the context that makes

---

[32] *Zhonghe ji*, 3.31a.

it possible to establish the relation between the two terms of the metonymy. They use, after all, a sort of code, but a code of which the key cannot be given, and which allows one to translate an image by means of a concept or of another image only within a given context. In a different context, the equivalence and the translation would be different. For this reason, the reader or the listener cannot establish a definitive code, and each time must rely on their comprehension of the spirit of the text rather than the letter of the text; and this is the stated purpose of the entire system. The Yin within the Yang, or true Yin, and the corresponding true Yang function are the entries in an encyclopedia that lead to a multitude of avenues, and as such they are treated by the authors.[33]

One of the most frequently used methods—which, on the plane of rhetoric, can be classified in the category of the ellipsis—consists in establishing a chain of generations, and in treating it as a chain of equivalences. This amounts to diversifying and, at the same time, intensifying; unfolding and, at the same time, contracting. On the one hand, one should proceed to the extraction—of the Yin within the Yang, and vice versa—and thus should generate, by distinguishing the internal from the external. On the other hand, the internal and the external are replaced in language with one another, as if they were identical.

Yu Yan offers an example of this procedure. The father of Metal, he says, is the Liquid Pearl, which is Mercury; it is so called because it moves and is unstable. This Liquid Pearl is in the Water, and thus forms the True Metal. Since Metal generates Water, the Liquid Pearl is the Mother of Water.[34] Thus the Liquid Pearl is the Mother of Water because it generates Metal that generates Water. A logical link is broken, so that the Liquid Pearl is both the Father of Metal and the Mother of Water, while Metal, according to tradition, generates Water. But the Liquid Pearl also "generates" Metal, because it purifies Metal in order to make the True Metal. In the same way, one can say that "within the Wood, Fire is born, which is Lead,"[35] because Fire purifies the Metal produced by Water to make the True Lead of the alchemists. This explains why Yu Yan continues by saying that Water

---

[33] See, for example, *Ziyang zhenren wuzhen zhizhi xiangshuo sansheng biyao*, 25b-33b.

[34] *Zhouyi cantong qi fahui*, 3.16a.

[35] *Ziyang zhenren wuzhen pian zhushu*, 4.16b.

generates the Metal that is Lead. Thus both Metal and Fire, two distinct instances, are Lead; and all of them are nothing but the only One Original Breath.

The processes of generation, gestation, conception, birth, and purification are perpetually confused in the language. "To receive one another, to be co-dependent, and to join are synonyms," says Yu Yan in an unequivocal way.[36] Mating and giving birth are one thing; union, completion, and generation are synonyms. By virtue of the principle that, in order for something to give birth to something else, it should in the first place contain it, "containing" is equivalent to "giving birth"; and the terms "transforming," "generating," and "containing," as well as "extracting," are interchangeable with one another.

Thus the Tiger is white because it pertains to Metal and to the West-Autumn, which are white; but, according to the traditional view, it generates the Water-Winter-North, which is black. Now, the Tiger begins its ascent from the North; therefore it emerges from the North-black, and is extracted from the enveloping North-black: the very North-black that it generates. Thus the white Tiger is black, and is born from what it gives birth to. By virtue of the fact that what is internal and is extracted from its external envelope is the true material of the alchemical Work, what is contained invades, as it is, the container, which in turn is identified with the contained, as we have seen earlier with regard to the Furnace.[37]

Another procedure consists in establishing two different systems as equivalent. The trigram Kan ☵, formed by two Yin lines that enclose a Yang line, is said to be male, while externally the Yin-female traits predominate. Being male, it corresponds to the "young Yang," i.e., to the Yang in its newly-born state. But Kan is also considered to be the Great Yin and is identified with Kun ☷, the trigram of pure Yin, because Kun gives birth to the young Yang.[38] Yu Yan says: "The first Yang is not born in Fu ䷗ (the hexagram of the newly-born Yang), but in Kun ䷁."[39] And again: "The Yang begins in Fu ䷗, the Yin ends in Kun ䷁: beginning and end coincide."[40] The trigram Kan exists there-

---

[36] *Zhouyi cantong qi fahui,* 5.2b.
[37] *Ziyang zhenren wuzhen pian zhushu,* 6.3a-b.
[38] *Zhonghe ji,* 3.26a.
[39] *Zhouyi cantong qi fahui,* 6.8b.
[40] *Zhouyi cantong qi fahui,* 6.10b.

fore on two distinct planes, and can play two different functions: Great Yin and young Yang. This results in its being located on the compass in two places, one pertaining to the system "prior to Heaven and Earth," i.e., the noumena (where it is placed in the West); and the other pertaining to the "posterior" system, which is the one of our phenomenal world (where it is placed in the North; see table 7). In fact, according to the chart of the first system, the trigram Kan is placed in the West, and Kun in the North; in the second, Kan is placed in the North. The two charts therefore are implicitly read transparently, one above the other, and the identity between Kan and Kun is implied. The white Tiger of the West is black, like the Water of the North.

Similarly, we see Li Daochun postulate that the South-West is Kun ☷ (this corresponds to its position in the chart "posterior to Heaven and Earth") and make of it the equivalent of the human body (as the complementary opposite of spirit). Then Li Daochun explains that Kun is the Yin containing Yang, while in the ordinary logic Kun is pure Yin, and it is Kan ☵ that contains the Yang. Thus, once again, Li Daochun establishes an equivalence between Kun and Kan, pure Yin and Yin containing Yang, "the mother and the child," as say other alchemists who conclude that the child generates the mother.

The alchemists' way of hustling the systems that they establish, or that they adopt as the foundation of their organization of the world, is highlighted in a sub-commentary to the *Wuzhen pian*.[41] This work explains that "the descending Breath of the Dragon is Fire, and the arising Breath of the Tiger is Water." This designates the Yin within the Yang that is Fire, and the Yang within the Yin that is Water. Then the text continues by saying: "In the Golden Tripod [that is Yin] there is Fire, which is the white Tiger"; and: "In the Jade Lake [that is Yang] there is Water, which is the green Dragon." This time, the Yang within the Yin is Fire, and vice versa—the opposite of what we have seen above. And the text concludes: "Yin and Yang have no fixed positions, Water and Fire are not fixed things; we use them in conjunction by inverting them; this system is wondrous and has no end," a sentence that can also be understood as meaning "this is the wondrous and infinite Principle." Thus we are clearly told that the mechanism that the alchemists attempt to play as a perpetual movement is intended to

[41] *Ziyang zhenren wuzhen pian zhushu*, 6.5b.

designate metaphorically the perpetual movement of life, of the world, and of the Dao.

On the plane of logic, we find again similar procedures that lead at the same time to observe the rules of a logical organization and to transgress them. The relations among the different terms are, in fact, clearly delimited, and can be perceived in the language used to designate them:

— Relation between container and contained: *bao*
— Relation of generation: *sheng*
— Relation of opposition, *ke*, or of contest: *zhan, xiangke*
— Relation of predominance: *zhi*
— Relation of different planes (cosmic, human, mental, physical, or "ontological"): *ben, ti*
— Relation of different "phenomenological" planes: *yong*

All these terms function as organizing factors. Other terms describe conventional differences, such as "is named" (*ming, hao,* or *wei*) and "borrows the name of" (*jiaming*); or indicate a transitional relation (such as *huawei*, "is transformed into"); or establish a relation between two languages or two systems of thought, of the type "A is a name of what Y calls B."

Now, all these relations can also be abolished between one sentence and the next one, or by a simple word (for example, *jia*: "figuratively," "occasionally," "conventionally"); or, in an even more drastic way, by a relation of pure equivalence, with a copula (*ji, wei, shi . . . ye*); or by a simple apposition.

The substitution by ellipsis or by what we might call rhetorical procedures, such as the synecdoche and the metonymy, are a rule both explicitly and implicitly. For example, Kun is pure Yin; but since Kun also gives birth to Yang, it is also the growing Yang, and this establishes an implicit equivalence between Yin and the growing Yang. Lead is the Dark Warrior, the Water of the North, and has a black color; but it is also and at the same time the white Tiger of the West, because the latter is extracted from the former.[42]

Moreover, the encasings and the generations are reciprocal (something that is conventionally inconceivable), and this is another way to

---

[42] *Longhu huandan jue,* 1a; and *Zhonghe ji,* 3.26a.

underline the notion of co-dependence (or, as a Buddhist would say, of "coarising"). Several patterns of relation that are abolished into a unity can be distinguished:

(1) Everything concentrates, *cuancu*, or merges into one: this is the simplest pattern.
(2) A recursive loop of the type "A generates B that generates A" or "that returns to A"; or "B, extracted from A, generates A":
    — from non-being, *wu*, to being, *you*, then again to non-being;[43]
    — from Water to Metal that generates Water;[44]
    — from Cinnabar to Metal, then again to Cinnabar;[45]
(3) An inversion of encasings: "A is produced from B that returns to A": the *xing* issues from the *ming* that returns to the *xing*.[46]
(4) The elements (two or four) are reciprocally encased into or generate one another.[47]

In the same way, there is no true difference between being, belonging to a category, being named, and becoming. In other words, we could say that "being," "having the name of" and "pertaining to" are equivalent. The substitutions are made, are possible, and are deemed to be legitimate both when there is an equivalence—marked by apposition or by a copula (*wei, ji, ye, shi*)—or when there is a relation of inclusion ("belonging to such category"), or a simple analogy or equivalence of language (metaphor or conventional denomination, *jia, ming*, which are deemed to be almost equivalent). These substitutions are also legitimate when two entities are joined by a relation of transition ("to transform into"); or when they exist on a double plane, for example ontological (*ben*, "fundamentally") and phenomenological (*yong*, "functionally").

Finally, what we call the "being" of something or someone is expressed by the relation of one thing to another. Thus what A "is" is also the distance that exists between A and B. And this can, in turn, be signified by the distance that separates or conjoins C to D. An aspect

---

[43] *Longhu huandan jue*, 1a.
[44] *Zhouyi cantong qi fenzhang tong zhenyi*, 2.23a.
[45] *Longhu huandan jue*, 1a, 4a, 6a.
[46] *Jindan zhizhi*, 3b.
[47] *Zhouyi cantong qi fenzhang tong zhenyi*, 2.17b, 22a, 23b; and *Danfang xuzhi*, 8a.

of A can also be defined under the form "A is to B what C is to D." Each term is the means and the end of other terms, their cause and their effect, and is related to them by a generative loop.

In parallel, a principle of economy is at play. Just like, technically, time in the Work can extend itself onto one year or one month, or condense itself into one day or one instant, so in the discourse the denominations and different relations among individual instances can be multiplied to the infinite, but can also be reduced to two, and finally to one.

This system of indefinite ellipses and encasings intends to describe the phenomenon of a Unity that is only realized through the very division that denies it—but that can only occur through it, and in which it cannot occur—in a mechanism that is incommensurable to logic and rationality, and is prior to language. Using this system, the alchemists use language and rationality by transgressing them, until they arrive one step before the extinction of communication. They introduce a doubt, a negation, a deep modulation that constitutes their assertion, their world. The intent of all their discourses is to speak not of complementary oppositions, and not even of the principle of symmetry that governs a good part of Chinese thought and its mode of expression—but to speak of encasings. This is why they insist so much on what they deem to be the "secret spring" of their art and of the entire cosmic mechanism: the presence of the Yin within the Yang and of the Yang within the Yin. This encasing is equivalent to its own negation: the expression of two contrary facts in one.

Role and Meaning of Numbers
in Taoist Cosmology and Alchemy

> "Thou hast ordered all things
> in measure and number and weight."
> *Book of Wisdom*, XI.20

> "He measured with his ray
> the boundaries of Heaven and Earth."
> *Ṛg-Veda*, VIII.25.18

INTRODUCTION

I will not dwell in this essay on the importance of numbers in China and on the role that numbers play in the Chinese civilization. Marcel Granet has examined these subjects at length in his *La pensée chinoise*, and I refer the reader to his discussion. I will not address either the role of numbers in divination, which is related to Taoism but is not specifically part of it. On the other hand, I will take into account several traditional data, to the extent to which the Taoist reflection on numbers and their manipulation is based on them.[1] It goes without saying that the limited scope of this essay will not permit an exhaustive presentation, and I will merely provide some of the main data.

---

[1] We can distinguish in this respect two main sources, even though in most cases they merge with one another: the school of Yin-Yang and the five agents (*yinyang wuxing*), on the one hand, and the *Yijing* (Book of Changes), on the other. The difference between them consists mainly in the distinction made in the *Yijing* between odd and even numbers, and in the speculations on the trigrams and the hexagrams related to the numbers. The influence of the *Yijing* is more clearly visible in internal alchemy, whose first certain traces date from the eighth century CE.

As we shall see in more detail, we can distinguish several functions performed by numbers in Taoism:

(1) Numbers are used to count, and therefore to date. In this sense, they include the sexagesimal cyclical signs known as "celestial stems" and "earthly branches," two groups of ten and twelve items, respectively, that existed at least since the Yin dynasty (see tables 8 and 9). The nature and function of these emblems are very similar to those of the numbers.[2]

(2) Numbers serve to distinguish and to group sets of items. In general, they emphasize the existence of a common element and make it possible to correlate those groups to one another, mainly on the basis of a single system of operation.[3] By doing so, numbers provide a model and, through this model and the correspondences that numbers can establish, they serve to build the "miniature worlds" (or microcosms) on which the Taoist works.[4]

---

[2] In the history of numbers inherited by the Taoists, an important role was played by the necessity, especially felt during the Han period, of harmonizing different spatiotemporal systems of reference with one another: the sexagesimal cyclical signs, the four seasons, the five agents, the first nine numbers that preside over a system of nonary distribution, the eight trigrams and the sixty-four hexagrams, the twelve months of the year, the twelve hours of the nycthemeron, the twelve pitch pipes, the twenty-four breaths (one per fortnight), the twenty-eight constellations of the zodiac, the seventy-two periods of five days of the year, and so forth. This was mainly the work of Meng Xi and Jing Fang in the first century BCE, and later of Zheng Xuan (127–200). They attempted to solve these issues by arranging those quantities or groups on the perimeters of concentric circles, in order to try to divide symmetrically, for example, what is counted by five and what is counted by twelve, even though the symmetry is sometimes inevitably broken by arranging them into groups of two or three. It seems to me that concern with computation arose mainly with regard to these issues.

[3] For example, numbers make it possible to connect temporal alternation and spatial distribution, and thus a rhythm with a place. They do so without any true idea of spatial measurement, but rather with regard to position, function, and quality.

[4] Numerology plays an important role in Taoist cosmology because it is one of the tools that establish relations between different domains (for example, the cosmos and the human body), which they also make *commensurable*. This is one of the foundations of analogy, which builds relations based

(3) Numbers assign a quality: for example, Yin or Yang, terrestrial or celestial, fullness, center, etc. Whether one takes into account their group of functioning or their quality, they establish affiliations, and therefore assign meanings.[5]

(4) The same number does not always have the same meaning.[6] Numbers obtained by addition or multiplication take their meanings according to the qualities of the numbers that produce them. As we shall see, their meanings vary according to how they deconstructed.

NUMBERS PRODUCE THE WORLD

Numerological cosmology

According to certain authors, the numbers preceded the "images" (*xiang*); according to others, it was the opposite. In either case, images and numbers are deemed to be primordial: they appeared before ideas or concepts, and before names and forms.[7] The *Zuozhuan* (late fourth century BCE) says that first there were the "images," related to the divination by the tortoise; then those images

---

on attributes or functions, and bridges the gaps between different areas in order to recover or introduce a unity of meaning. The "measures" established by the numbers are one form of these analogies. They make it possible to constitute something similar to "blocks" of thought that provide organizing structures.

[5] In addition, numbers can make symmetry apparent; for example, the symmetry between right and left, above and below, and Yin and Yang. The articulation of thought then is made by means of references to images and structures symmetrically arranged. This acquires the value of a convincing picture of reality, and therefore of a demonstration.

[6] For example, we shall distinguish between Two in the sense of couple, of duality, of division, of duplication, and of second; between Three in the sense of fusion of two into one, of a hierarchical triad, etc.

[7] There are exceptions to this statement; the *Zhong Lü chuandao ji* (Records of the Transmission of the Dao from Zhongli Quan to Lü Dongbin), for example, places the appearance of forms before the appearance of numbers. See *Xiuzhen shishu*, 14.9a.

multiplied themselves and generated the numbers, associated with the milfoil.[8] Taoist authors often quote this statement.[9]

The use of numbers to represent the world in its multiple aspects and distributions is a fundamental feature of the science of *xiangshu* ("images and numbers"). This science is intimately linked to the exegesis of the *Yijing* (Book of Changes), and it is well known that the Taoists have drawn from it. The arithmetic manipulation of numbers was intended to account for the structure of situations and their changes, and thus to make the world understandable: knowing the structure of numbers results in a better comprehension of the world. In this respect, the Taoists are fully in line with this tradition.

For the Chinese, and especially for the Taoists, the numbers produce the world. In the words of a fourteenth-century Taoist commentator:

> Heaven and Earth circulate and operate by numbers, and the ten thousand beings are born by numbers. The numbers are the movement and the rest of Yin and Yang in the Great Ultimate (*Taiji*).[10]

According to Yuanyang zi, the numbers are spirits.[11] For the *Hunyuan bajing zhenjing* (True Scripture of the Eight Luminous Spirits of the Inchoate Origin), when the numbers of Fire and Water were "complete" (*manzu*) they began to "coalesce into chaos" and "the One Breath of the cosmos emerged" (here the numbers come even before Unity); when the numbers of Yin and Yang and the Sun and the Moon were complete, stars and constellations were born; when the numbers of the revolutions of Yin and Yang and the five agents were complete, they could reach accomplishment; and the same is true of the alchemical Work, where each of the five agents must attain the fullness of its number.[12]

The notion of the "complete" state of numbers is complemented by the notion of their "exhaustion," which marks the end of the

---

[8] Couvreur, *La chronique de la Principauté de Lou*, vol. I, p. 306.

[9] See, for example, *Daode zhenjing jiyi*, 2.6b; and *Zhouyi cantong qi zhu*, 3.14a.

[10] *Wenchang dadong xianjing*, 1.13a.

[11] *Yuanyang zi jinye ji*, 10a.

[12] For these four statements, see *Hunyuan bajing zhenjing*, 1.1a, 1.1b, 1.2a, and 4.2a-3b, respectively.

world.[13] Obviously, these notions are based on ideas of cosmic cycles and of times of maturation and decline; they pertain to the ancient arithmology associated with divination and to the cosmic arithmology that accompanied it. However, while the numbers applied to these cycles express a course in time, they concurrently attest to a state (more or less young, mature, or old), a configuration in space, a structure. A number does not measure a quantity: it indicates a moment, a sequence, and a point in a configuration. In other words, numbers assign a position within time and space; time and space, in turn, provide the setting for the manifestation of possibilities, and by doing so they assign a quality and a relation. Their function is both to mark a difference, a discontinuity (differences in quality and space), and at the same time to ensure continuity in the form of a sequence.

Therefore numbers account for the order of the world. They represent an organic and hierarchical order that is the foundation of the work done by the Taoist adept who, in his role of demiurge, is similar to the mythical emperor, Yu the Great: he measures Heaven and Earth, places markers on them, and organizes them. With the "images," the numbers are one of the tools that make this work possible.

Numerological cosmogonies

According to different authors, the One is either identified with the Dao or—following Laozi—regarded as being produced by the Dao. These perspectives are not mutually exclusive, but are complementary. They correspond to two conceptions of the One: on the one hand, the metaphysical One, which is not a number;[14] on the other, the One as the producer, which as such is the first number.[15] Typically, One—the origin of life—is the number assigned to Water, and therefore to the Yin principle, as the first element, the origin of all things; in this case, One is deemed to be a Yin number.[16] This is the general rule in Taoist

---

[13] *Taishang miaoshi jing*, 1b.

[14] See Solomon, "'One is no Number' in China and the West."

[15] I will not dwell on this point, which would require an extended discussion and will be the subject of a separate study. [See Isabelle Robinet, "Un, deux, trois: Les différentes modalités de l'Un et sa dynamique," *Cahiers d'Extrême-Asie* 8 (1995): 175–220. — Ed.]

[16] See *Zhouyi cantong qi*, 1.35a.

texts. In contrast to it, the exegetical schools of the *Yijing* assign number One to Qian ☰, the Origin, pure Yang, and Heaven; in this case, the origin of the world is the movement that pertains to Yang.

The One as producer of the world reflects the fundamental monism of the Chinese: the world is the effect of the unfolding of the One into multiplicity. The transition to multiplicity occurs by the intermediation of the Two ("The One generates the Two," says Laozi), represented by what the *Yijing* calls "the two Principles" (*liangyi*). With few exceptions, this expression designates Yin and Yang, the bipolarity, the existence of two extreme poles whose tension and mutual attraction support the dynamism of the world. At the origin of the world, in this case, is the Two, as in the Heaven-Earth couple. Two is duality. But in another sense, it is the number of Yin, of Kun ☷, and of the Earth. It comes second after the One, which is the number of Yang, of Qian, and of Heaven. This is the Two seen as discontinuity; it is the broken line of the *Yijing*, opposite to the solid line of the One, the Yang. Two also means duplication: according to a general interpretation that has no historical truth but is symbolically meaningful, the original trigrams were later doubled to form the hexagrams. Duplication pertains to the earthly Two, and means that we enter the world of phenomena.

In Taoism, generally—and again following Laozi—the Two generates the Three (and not the Four, as it does, for example, in the *Yijing* and in Shao Yong). According to a famous sentence in the calendrical chapter of the *Hanshu* (History of the Former Han Dynasty; chapter 21A), often referred to by the Taoists, the Three is contained within the One of the Great Ultimate (*Taiji*). It represents the agreement of the two complementary forces, Yin and Yang, and their product. It is the sign of the unity restored after the separation that establishes the world: on the one hand, the binary fission; on the other, the fertility of the union of the complementary opposites. The Three is Harmony, agreement, the Son, Man, or the human world, produced by Heaven and Earth, a mingling of Yin and Yang. Thus the Three is a replica of the primordial Unity from which, as Laozi says, all things are born. In short, it is Unity in its productive aspect. This is well expressed as early as the Han period in texts that include the *Huainan zi* (140 BCE) and the *Taiping jing* (late Han, revised in the fourth century?). Both texts deem this to be a fundamental aspect of things.[17]

Five is the number of the center. According to a tradition that dates at least from the Han period, inherited by Taoism and by several other traditions of that time, Five divides the "emergent" or "generative" numbers (*sheng*), which go from One to Four and add up to Ten, from the "achieved" numbers (*cheng*), which go from Six to Nine (see table 4).[18] Five is the number of the traditional agents, corresponding to the four cardinal points and the Center; in this respect, it represents the presence of the Center added to the Four. But Five has also designated a spatiotemporal device related to the changing seasons and to the action of the five agents, the fifth of which plays the role of a catalyst or of a central dynamic force.

Several Taoist texts describe the formation of the world in terms of the growth of numbers. I will quote only one example:

> Yin and Yang have established the Three Powers (Heaven, Earth, Man) and have divided themselves into Four images (*xiang*, cardinal points or trigrams); the Four images have unfolded into Five agents; the Five agents have generated Six pitch pipes (*lü*); the Six pitch pipes have divided themselves into Seven rectors;[19] the Seven rectors have transformed themselves into Eight trigrams; the Eight trigrams have produced eight times eight, that is, Sixty-four

[17] It is due the nature of this number that thirty days, or three hundred days, or three years are required for a practice to be considered "complete" or "full" (*bei* or *man*). See, for example, *Hunyuan bajing zhenjing*, 5.12a. The division of the world into three fundamental levels—Heaven, Earth, and Man—remained essential throughout Taoist cosmology of all ages and trends, even when concepts and formulations changed. For example, in an alchemical text of the Song period, the *Zhong Lü chuandao ji*, we find this statement: "One is the constitutive body (*ti*), Two is its functioning (*yong*), Three is the creation (*zaohua*). Creation entirely relies on the union [of Yin and Yang]. Above, in the middle, and below are the three Powers: Heaven, Earth, and Man" (*Xiuzhen shishu*, 14.8a). In this sense, Three is significant both of hierarchy and of correspondence between vertically arranged planes.

[18] I adopt here the terminology of Kalinowski, *Cosmologie et divination dans la Chine ancienne*. [The original French terms are "naissant," "generatif," and "performatif." — Ed.]

[19] Usually deemed to be the Sun, the Moon, and the five planets.

hexagrams; each hexagram has six divine lines, making altogether 384 lines.[20]

However, the Taoists have also appropriated the system of the *Qian zuodu* (Opening the Way to the Understanding of Qian ☰),[21] which is quoted in the first chapter of the *Liezi* (third-fourth century CE; date uncertain, and made of various historical layers). In this system, the One appears after a sequence of several chaotic states (the so-called "four greats"), and therefore after a slow maturation process; then it generates the Seven, and then the Nine.[22] This refers to the computation of the *Yijing*, where Seven and Nine are the numbers of young and old Yang, respectively. In this system, Nine (a number that will be discussed more at length below) is the last of the prime numbers (1 to 9), their "exhaustion" (*jiu*, a play on words that ties this term to the word *jiu*, meaning "nine"), after which the computation returns to the Unity. Nine therefore means the accomplished Totality, the completion.

In the same vein, and in agreement with the calendrical chapter of the *Hanshu* and with the numerology of the *Yijing*, certain Shangqing texts have adopted Six and Nine as the extreme numbers of Yin and Yang. Thus there are two ends of the world, one due to the Six-Yin, the other to the Nine-Yang.[23]

The odd numbers play an essential role among the prime numbers: "The numbers emerge in One, are established in Three, are accomplished in Five, flourish in Seven, and culminate in Nine," says a text of the ancient Lingbao.[24] This passage attests to the consideration given to the tradition of the *Yijing*, which draws a fundamental distinction between the Yang odd numbers and the Yin even numbers.

---

[20] *Hunyuan bajing zhenjing*, 4.8a-b.

[21] An "apocryphon" (*weishu*) on the *Yijing*, dating from the Han period.

[22] The "four greats" (*sitai*) are the Great Simplicity (*Taiyi*), the Great Beginning (*Taichu*), the Great Commencement (*Taishi*), and the Great Purity (*Taisu*). Later they became five with the addition of the Great Ultimate (*Taiji*). See Robinet, "The Place and Meaning of the Notion of *Taiji* in Taoist Sources prior to the Ming Dynasty."

[23] See Robinet, *La révélation du Shangqing dans l'histoire du taoïsme*, vol. I, p. 139.

[24] *Taishang Lingbao tiandi yundu ziran miaojing*, 1a-b.

According to one text, the longevity of the cosmos is consumed with the depletion of numbers 3, 5, 7, and 9.[25]

The cosmic numbers 25 (the sum of the first odd numbers) for Heaven and 30 (the sum of the even numbers) for the Earth, whose total is 55, has also been adopted by Taoist speculation. This is especially true for the milieux of the alchemists, who drew these numbers from the *Xici*, the "Great Appendix" to the *Yijing*. A thirteenth-century Taoist text clearly and concisely outlines the principles, at that time already widespread, governing these numbers:

> In Heaven and on Earth, there is no number without use. As for 1, 3, 5, 7, 9, they are Yang odd numbers; the number of Heaven is 25. As for 2, 4, 6, 8, 10, they are Yin even numbers; the number of the Earth is 30. The total is 55, "the number of Heaven and Earth." We obtain 50, "the number of the great expansion," by removing 5, which is the root of the five agents. We use 49 [yarrow stalks for divination], because again we remove 1 to symbolize the motion-less Great Ultimate (*Taiji*). Thus we know that there is a constitutive basis (*ti*, the One) and an operation (*yong*).[26]

Reversal of order

In terms of numbers, as we have said, the world is produced by the unfolding of the One into multiplicity. Hence, by going backward through the numbers, one goes back in time. This is the view expressed by the *Xianquan ji* (Anthology of Mountain Springs) when it states that by going backward (*ni*, turning to the right), one knows what has not yet been born, while by going in the "right" sense (*shun*, turning to the left), one knows what has been born.[27] Turning to the left means going in the sense of Yang and in the direction of the growth of numbers. Vice versa, turning to the right means going in the sense of Yin and in the direction of the decrease of numbers: this is the course of the Yin numbers—from 8, young Yin, to 6, old Yin—in the system of the *Yijing*.

---

[25] *Taishang miaoshi jing*, 1b.

[26] *Xiuzhen shishu*, 9.6b.

[27] *Xianquan ji*, 1.27a. [On this subject see also the essay entitled "The World Upside Down in Taoist Internal Alchemy" in the present volume. — Ed.]

The *dunjia* (Hidden Stem) method, which allows an adept to become invisible and disappear, enjoins marching forward on the magic square until number 6 for the celestial, generative numbers, and then backward for the earthly, achieved numbers.[28] This can be compared to the arrangement of the Eight Trigrams known as "prior to Heaven" (and Earth, i.e., pre-cosmic), which places the numbers around a circle in a sequence going from top to bottom and from right to left for the Yang trigrams, then again from top to bottom, but from left to right for the Yin trigrams (see table 7).[29] This arrangement pertains to the generation of the trigrams and the world, and is juxtaposed to the one "posterior to Heaven." Here numbers are assigned to the trigrams so that one goes from the youngest one to the second born and to the eldest one, then returns to Gen ☶ (symbol of a pause), and finally reaches Kun ☷ and Qian ☰. In this way, starting from the phenomenal post-cosmic state, one goes back through time.[30]

The Taoists therefore begin by setting a sequence of numbers that represent the unfolding of the One into the world toward multiplicity, then return to the One by going back through time. This is one meaning of the reversal of the generation order of the five agents (see table 3). Li Daochun (fl. ca. 1290) advocates this meaning when, having reminded the words of Laozi, "The One generates the Two, the Two generates the Three, the Three generates the ten thousand beings" (*Daode jing*, 42), he adds: "The ten thousand beings hold the Three, the Three returns to the Two, and the Two returns to the One."[31] Chen Zhixu (1290–ca. 1368) quotes the same sentence, saying that this is the meaning of "going backward" (*ni*).[32]

NUMEROLOGICAL CORRESPONDENCES

Number Three is the origin of the human world in the Chinese tradition, but is also the origin of the celestial world in Taoist cosmology. The Three Primes (Sanyuan) or Three Sovereigns (Sanhuang)

[28] See Schipper and Wang Hsiu-huei, "Progressive and Regressive Time Cycles in Taoist Ritual."
[29] *Zhouyi tu*, 1.9a-b; *Dadan zhizhi*, 2.12b-13a.
[30] *Dadan zhizhi*, 2.13a.
[31] *Zhonghe ji*, 2.5a-b.
[32] *Shangyang zi jindan dayao*, 4.7b.

recall the three mythical emperors of China; in Taoism, however, they are gods. They generate the three supreme deities, the three Lords who rule in the three Heavens and whose Breaths, also three in number, have created the world.[33] Confirming that Three is a replica of the primordial One, the Three Primes or three Breaths are said to be One. They give birth to Yin, Yang, and Harmony, or, at a different level, to Heaven, Earth, and Man.[34]

In the cosmos, this triad is replicated by the three luminaries (Sun, Moon, and stars), and in man, by the three major deities of the body (*sanyuan*), one for each of the parts in which the body is vertically divided.[35] The three components of the human being, whose order of precedence (from the lowest or most gross to the highest or most subtle one) varies according to different schools—essence, spirit, and breath; or essence, breath, and spirit—are also correlated with the Triad-One, the foundation of the world.[36] The notion of the Triad-One presides over various forms of meditation, where adepts are enjoined to "preserve the Three-One" who, being "eternal, nameless, and chaotic," is equated with the Dao or with Unity, the ultimate Truth. The Taoists have also applied the Mādhyamika dialectic to these two numbers, Three and One, in order to account for their interpenetration and identity.[37]

Three is closely related to Five already since mythical history, with the Three Sovereigns and the Five Emperors. The Taoists have placed great importance on these two numbers and on their association with one another. In general, Three marks a vertical distribution of the

---

[33] The three Lords are of those of Heaven (Tianbao jun), of the Numinous Treasure (Lingbao jun), and of Spirit (Shenbao jun).

[34] Robinet, *Les commentaires du Tao tö king jusqu'au VIIe siècle*, pp. 149–73.

[35] These are the abdomen, corresponding to the Earth; the thorax, associated with Man; and the head, related to Heaven.

[36] Robinet, *Les commentaires du Tao tö king*, pp. 174–90.

[37] *Id.*, pp. 198–202. This conception of the Three is referred to in a Taoist ritual text when it states that the Three is the "ancestral" breath, while the One is the "emerging" breath; see *Daofa huiyuan*, 65.4a. This designates the One as producer, as discussed above. In the oldest texts, dating from the fifth century, this One corresponds to the notion of a deified Laozi born of the union of the three Breaths, and representing the single principle of the multiple Taoist doctrines. See Robinet, *Les commentaires du Tao tö king*, pp. 168–69.

world (above, below, and middle), while Five marks a horizontal division (four quadrants and center). With regard to physiology, Five designates the five viscera, which match the five planets, the five cardinal mountains, and of course the five agents—Water, Wood, Fire, Soil, and Metal—as well as the entire system of correspondences that is presided over by the five agents in the Chinese tradition. Other distinctions by five were made at the human level: an anonymous commentator of the *Cantong qi* (Token for Joining the Three), for example, distinguishes five celestial odd numbers, which correspond to idea (*yi*), breath (*qi*), will (*zhi*), wisdom (*hui*), and knowledge (*zhi*); and five Yin even numbers, which correspond to the four limbs and the entire body.[38]

Four is the number of the Earth, and the same is true of its twin, Eight. The cardinal points are four, and the points of the compass, eight. The eight points consist of eight "gates" that were correlated with the eight trigrams in the first century CE by the *Shuogua* (Explanation of the Trigrams), an appendix of the *Yijing*. However, under the influence of Buddhism, the texts of the ancient Lingbao (late fourth to early fifth centuries) began to use the number Ten to count the directions: the eight points of the compass with the addition of above and below.[39]

As was noted by Granet,[40] the classification system by Six was important in China, and the Taoists partly maintained it. The Chinese tradition recognized a division of space by six, as shown, for example, by the *Zhuangzi* with its frequent mentions of the six conjunctions and the six poles (*liuhe* and *liuji*); by the *Yijing* with the six positions of the hexagrams lines (*liuwei*); and the by *Yuanyou* (Far Roaming) with the "six barren lands" (*liumo*).[41] At the same time,

---

[38] *Zhouyi cantong qi zhu*, 3.14b.

[39] Ten, as well as its multiples, sometimes represents a totality by itself. Ten is also the "achieved" number of the agent Soil, which is the center. However, this number in China has never had the importance that the Greeks and the Kabbalah granted to it: in general, in China, a totality is represented by Nine.

[40] Granet, *La pensée chinoise*, pp. 104 and 311.

[41] Contrary to what was suggested by Erik Zürcher ("Buddhist Influence on Early Taoism: A Survey of Scriptural Evidence," p. 124), Six owes nothing to Buddhism. However, this number is rarely incorporated into Taoism, except for a few Shangqing texts such as the *Shangqing waiguo fangpin*

there are six cosmic breaths;[42] they are matched by the six breaths in man, which are six ways of breathing used in certain Taoist practices. In addition, the five viscera are coupled with six other organs, called *fu* ("receptacles"). Qualitatively, Six is the number of great Yin, and as such is the number of the Moon.[43] In the context of the sexagesimal computation that goes back to the Yin dynasty, the Taoists have deified the Six Jia (*liujia*), named after the first celestial cyclical sign, and the Six Ding (*liuding*), the sign of the South and Fire. In the speculations of internal alchemy focused on the *Yijing*, Six acquires importance as the number of the hexagram lines; it also designates the three "sons" and the three "daughters," namely, the six trigrams generated by the first two, Qian and Kun.

Furthermore, Six and Eight are Yin numbers. As a relatively late text explains, Six "is the number of great Yin, because it is the central number of the Yin numbers, 2, 4, 6, 8, and 10."[44] Traditionally, Eight is more particularly the number of the Earth with its eight gates (the eight points of the compass), corresponding to the eight trigrams. With regard to time, the "eight joints" (*bajie*) are the first days of each season, the equinoxes, and the solstices, all of which are important dates in the Taoist liturgical time. The luminous celestial spirits (*jing*) residing in the body are also counted in groups of eight.

Seven is the number of rising Yang. It appears in the Shangqing texts, for example to combine the horizontal plane, consisting of five points, with above and below; or to add Yin and Yang to the five agents. The same view is applied to the pantheon, where the Father above and the Mother below are added to the spirits of the five viscera. In physiology, the five viscera are supplemented by the *ying* and the *wei*, the two systems of "construction" and "defense," to obtain the number seven.

Qingtong neiwen (fourth century CE?), with its six "outer realms" distributed on the basis of the traditional five with the addition of the top. See also *Dongzhen Shangqing shenzhou qizhuan qibian wutian jing*, 2a-b.

[42] Wind, heat, moisture, fire, drought, and cold. According to the *Taishang huadao dushi xianjing*, 11a, instead, the six breaths are the five agents and wind.

[43] *Zhouyi cantong qi fahui*, 2.16b-17a. It is probably in its function as the number of great Yin that Six has been attached to the baleful Heavens that Zhang Daoling had to drive away, and replace by the nine heavens (a Yang number). Later, those six heavens became hells.

[44] *Zhouyi tu*, 3.21a-b.

Nine is a number as fundamental as Five in Chinese cosmology. As we have said, is the last of the prime numbers. It is also the sum of the first three odd numbers, as noted in an alchemical text.[45] Nine therefore marks a culmination, a totality; but it also indicates a rebirth, because everything is constantly repeated. It refers to the division of the cosmos into nine sectors associated with the myth of Yu the Great, who divided China into nine regions; to the nine sections of the *Hongfan* (The Great Plan); and to the ancient liturgy of the Mingtang (Hall of Light), of which two variants seem to have existed: a quinary one and a nonary one, the latter reproducing the nonary arrangement of the altar of Three Sovereigns.[46]

Nine has a special celestial connotation for the Taoists, and its role in the formation of the world is analogous to the role of the Three.[47]

---

[45] *Huizhen ji*, 1.3a.

[46] See Lagerwey, *Taoist Ritual in Chinese Society and History*, 26. While the arrangement by Five concerns the circulation and the alternation of the five agents, the one by Nine refers to the movement of the stellar god Taiyi, who is associated with the speculations on the *Yijing* and therefore to the milieux of the diviners and the Han apocrypha, and was adopted by the Taoists. As Marc Kalinowski recapitulates, the quinary system "is structured around phases, sectors, and seasons, while the other (i.e., the nonary system) is structured around primes numbers, palaces, and trigrams"; see Kalinowski, "La transmission du dispositif des Neuf Palais sous les Six-Dynasties," p. 805. The synthesis between these two systems was made during the Six Dynasties and occurred in Taoist circles, as Kalinowski has shown (*ibid.*).

[47] The Shangqing texts, for example, maintain that the three Breaths that established the world subdivided themselves into nine, which in turn created the nine heavens. These seem to be, in fact, the nine heavens instituted by Zhang Daoling; see Robinet, *La révélation du Shangqing*, vol. II, p. 90, and *Taishang Dongxuan Lingbao Tianzun shuo Luotian dajiao shangpin miaojing*, 1a. The nine heavens, of course, occurred before the "eight directions" (*id.*, 2a). The regions of Earth, like those of Heaven, are counted by nine, and the same is true of the layers—or rather, the meanders—of the underground hells, which are matched by the nine coils of the intestines. Nine also are the stars of the Northern Dipper (two of which are invisible), and nine are the openings in the human body, and in the heart of the Sage. When the revolutions of Heaven reach the number of 9,900, the numbers of the nine heavens are "exhausted," and the end of the world ensues; see Robinet, *La révélation du Shangqing*, vol. I, p. 139. Nine to the power of 2, which makes Eighty-one, is the "fundamental number" (*tishu*) of the Yang breath, while Six to the power of 2 is the number of the Yin breath. Similarly, the blood (Yin) of girls measures 36 "bushels" (*dou*), and the breath (Yang) of boys, when it

It is the number of birth or rebirth: nine months are necessary for the gestation of the ordinary human embryo or the new body of the Taoist; and nine transmutations are required for compounding the Elixir. The god of the Original Commencement (Yuanshi) measures 90,000,000 *zhang*, and wears a headgear of nine lights and a sash of nine colors.[48] The god Laozi took 81 years to be born; he transforms himself nine times, and has nine names and 81 esoteric signs on his body.[49]

Number Ten divides the directions of the world in Buddhism (eight, with the addition of above and below), and was adopted by Lingbao under Buddhist influence. The recitation of the *Duren jing* (Scripture on Salvation) in the heavens by the supreme deity at the dawn of time is performed ten times for the ten directions. Ten, therefore, would seem to be a number adopted especially within the Lingbao circles. In the more purely Chinese tradition, it is mainly related to the celestial cyclical signs and to the Sun.[50] It is also in the tenth month, after nine months of gestation, that a child is born. Unlike other numbers, nevertheless, Ten plays virtually no role in the systems of correspondence.

Twelve and its multiples have been important in Taoism, especially in the circles of the Celestial Masters and their institutions. According to traditional Chinese cosmology, 12 is the number of the earthly cyclical signs, or "branches"; 12 are the marks (*chen*) of Heaven; 12 are the months of the year; and 24 are the "breaths of the year," one per fortnight. Modeling himself on these numbers, Zhang Daoling established 24 dioceses, in imitation, according to the legend, of

---

reaches its maximum (at the age of 15), has a length of 810 feet. See *Xishan qunxian huizhen ji*, 3.10a. Original Breath runs 810 *zhang* per day. The "pure room" (the meditation chamber of the Taoists) must measure 81 feet because this is the number of the rising Yang breath; see Chen Guofu, *Daozang yuanliu kao*, p. 334. 90,000 *li* ("miles") divide Heaven from Earth and each star of the Dipper from one another; *Taishang Lingbao tiandi yundu ziran miaojing*, 1a-b (text belonging to the ancient Lingbao, and therefore dating from the late fourth-early fifth centuries CE). The Sun has nine rays inhabited by spirits.

[48] *Shangqing yuanshi bianhua baozhen shangjing jiuling taimiao Guishan xuanlu*, 1.10a-b.

[49] Seidel, *La divinisation de Lao tseu dans le Taoïsme des Han*, pp. 96–97, 100.

[50] See, for example, *Zhouyi cantong qi fahui*, 2.16b-17a.

Isabelle Robinet

Emperor Gaozu who had sacrificed in 24 parishes to respond to the 24 breaths. In fact, Zhang Daoling is also said to have sacrificed 24 oxen in 24 locations where he established 24 altars.[51] Each of the nine offices of the Three Primes are occupied by 120 officers, and their regulations consist of 1,200 paragraphs.[52] In addition, 24 is the sum of the odd prime numbers, 3, 5, 7, and 9, which constantly recur in the texts. As part of the correspondence between different cosmic planes, the 24 parishes of the Celestial Masters were correlated with 24 (later 28) constellations, 24 gods of the human body, 24 categories of predestined people, 24 hells, and so forth.[53]

Twenty-seven (3x9) has sometimes been taken into account, but less frequently. The *Sandong zhunang* (Pearl Satchel of the Three Caverns) devotes a section to it, with 27 types of immortals, 27 immortal high officials (*dafu*), and 27 "Lords of the Living Breaths of the Body."[54] Another text mentions 27 spirits of the body. This number, therefore, seems to be used only to count immortals or deities, due to its being obtained from 3 and 9.

Thirty-six is used in conjunction with the 360 days of the year (the number 365 is also sometimes used, but involves complex calculations). They are matched by 36 bodily joints in Taoist physiology, 36 symbols conferred at ordination, 36 steps on the ladder of knives that a Taoist climbs during his initiation, 36 heavens, and so forth. The 36,000 "external" spirits of three different kinds, numbering 12,000 each, are matched by 36,000 "internal" spirits.[55]

One text describes the formation of the human body in terms of numbers, after doing the same in terms of organs. The Three burners (*sanjiao*) generate the Eight arteries (*mo*), which generate the Twelve vessels (*luo*), which in turn generate 180 related vessels, which generate 180 other vessels, which generate 36,000 other vessels, which generate 365 bones, which generate 84,000 pores (as we shall see, 84 is

[51] *Guang hongming ji*, 171b, and *Falin biezhuan*, 208a-b.
[52] *Taizhen Yudi siji mingke jing*, 1.8a. As is well known, the ecclesiastical administration of the Celestial Masters sought to model itself on the official administration; *Dengzhen yinjue*, 3.11b. In particular, the Celestial Masters modeled themselves on the Zhou administration, which had 120 as its ideal number, and regulated itself on Heaven with its three dukes, nine great ministers, 27 high dignitaries, and 81 officers, forming a total of 120.
[53] *Sandong zhunang*, 7.6a-7b and 22b ff.
[54] *Id.*, 7.22a-24b.
[55] *Hunyuan bajing zhenjing*, 4.8b and 5.3a-b.

a number inherited from Buddhism that defines the distance between Heaven and Earth).[56] These numbers are obviously symbolic, and are intended to relate the body to the cosmos.

The cosmic numbers 25 for Heaven and 30 for the Earth have also been associated with Taoist physiology. Number 25 is obtained by the addition of the 9 orifices, 5 viscera, 6 *fu* organs, and 5 officers (*guan*) of the whole body. Number 30 is the sum of the 20 fingers of the hands and the feet, the 8 bones, and the two kidneys.[57] Number 50 is obtained in a similar way.

The Shangqing deities are 72 or 74: three times three groups of eight, with the addition of the original Father and Mother.[58] The *hou* also are traditionally 72; this term defines a period of five days (or five and a half days when the year is counted as having 365 days). In addition to his 81 physical signs, the god Laozi has 72 other signs.

As we have said, by virtue of these correspondences one is enabled to create a microcosm—for example, the alchemical crucible. A famous stanza of the *Cantong qi* assigns symbolic numbers to the dimensions of the tripod: the circumference should measure 3.5 (explained by commentators as equivalent to one foot and five inches, i.e., 1.5); the "mouth," 4.8; the height, 12 feet; and so forth. Other versions, such as the one found in the *Xiudan miaoyong zhili lun* (Treatise on the Ultimate Principles of the Wondrous Operation of the Cultivation of the Elixir), are based on different reference points. The altar has four sides for the four seasons. It has three stages, each of which has a height of 1.2 feet to correspond to the twelve months and the twelve double hours; the width of the lower stage must measure 3.6 *zhang* for the 36 periods; the width of the median stage, 2.4 *zhang* for the 24 hours; and the width of the higher stage, 1.6 *zhang*, which makes 2x8 = 1 pound (see below on symbolism of these numbers). The tripod must measure 3 feet to correspond to Heaven, Earth, and Man; and it must contain nine "palaces" for the nine stars of the Northern Dipper.[59]

[56] *Xishan qunxian huizhen ji*, 3.1b.

[57] *Zhouyi cantong qi zhu*, 3.14b.

[58] See Robinet, *La révélation du Shangqing*, vol. I, p. 126.

[59] *Xiudan miaoyong zhili lun*, 9b. See also, for example, *Shangyang zi jindan dayao tu*, 8b; Ho Ping-yü and Needham, "The Laboratory Equipment of the Early Medieval Chinese Alchemist," pp. 66–67; and Sivin, "The Theoretical Background of Elixir Alchemy," pp. 279–80.

Isabelle Robinet

COMBINATIONS AND DECONSTRUCTIONS

Most numbers that play a role in numerology can be deconstructed in different ways, and accordingly take different meanings. The deconstruction into other significant numbers is performed mainly on the basis of the subdivision between Yang or celestial odd numbers (1, 3, 5, 7, 9), and Yin or earthly even numbers (2, 4, 6, 8, and possibly 10). For the Earth, for example, 32 = 4x8; for Heaven, 81 = 9x9. The meaning of a number depends on how it is deconstructed.

Combinations of different numbers are often accompanied by an exchange of attributes. Let us first look at the numbers associated with the five agents (see tables 1 and 2).[60] As seen already in the *Hanshu*, each agent is assigned an "emergent" or "generative" number and an "achieved" number. This is combined with the system of the *Xici*, where a distinction is drawn between earthly and celestial numbers. Thus, each agent has a celestial odd number and an earthly even number. In addition, while number One is celestial, it is matched to Water, which pertains to the Yin principle; vice versa, the Yang-Fire is matched to number Two, which is earthly. This exchange of attributes is at the basis of the formation of the world.

Three can be seen as consisting of Two, the Yin and the Yang, with the addition of the *yi* of the *Yijing* that counts as One;[61] or as One for Water, Two for Fire, and Three for their conjunction.[62] Six is deconstructed into 3+3, the three Yin and three Yang trigrams generated by Qian ☰ and Kun ☷; or into the sum of the "emergent" Yin numbers, 4+2. Five is the sum of the numbers assigned in internal alchemy to the North (1) and the West (4), and of those assigned to the South (2) and the East (3). The sum of these numbers, with the addition of the number of Soil (5), gives 15. This number therefore is the equivalent of 3 times 5, "the combination of numbers that establishes life."[63] This computation acquires great importance in internal alchemy,

---

[60] According to a fundamental principle that is often reminded in Taoist texts, Heaven with the One formed Water, Earth with the Two formed Fire, Heaven with the Three formed Wood, Earth with the Four formed Metal, Heaven with the Five formed Soil, Earth with the Six formed Water, Heaven with the Seven formed Fire, Earth with the Eight formed Wood, Heaven with the Nine formed Metal, and Earth with the Ten formed Soil.

[61] *Xiuzhen shishu*, 9.1b, version of the thirteenth century.

[62] *Zhouyi cantong qi zhu*, 1.20b.

[63] *Taigu ji*, 3.7b.

where the three Fives should be reduced to One, a point on which the *Wuzhen pian* ("Regulated Verses," poem 14) and many later writers and commentators insist. But a commentary to the *Cantong qi* composed before the year 962 arrives to number 15 by a different calculation, adding the sums of the Yin and Yang "achieved" numbers, namely, 7+8 and 9+6.[64]

Similarly, Twelve is formed by the addition of Nine, the number of the East, and Three, the number of the South in the system of the "induced sounds" (*nayin*); but it is also formed by the addition of Seven for the West and Five for the North in the same system. In this case Twelve, and not Five, represents the coupling of the two Yin and the two Yang cardinal points.[65] Twelve, though, is also deconstructed as the sum of the six "male" and the six "female" pitch pipes. It is found, moreover, in the form of 10+2 with regard to the measure of the large intestine, namely one *zhang* (equivalent to ten feet) and two feet, corresponding to the twelve hours of the day. The small intestine, instead, measures two *zhang* and four feet, corresponding to the twenty-four breaths of the year.[66]

The description of the mountain of hell in the *Daofa huiyuan* (Collected Essentials of Taoist Methods) combines several symbolic numbers. Its height is 36,000 *li* ("miles"), and its circumference is 5,000 *li*. On the mountain and below are twelve palaces, each measuring 10,000 *li* in circumference; and on each side of these palaces there are six more palaces, making altogether 24 palaces (6x4, Yin numbers). However, 24 can also be considered as the sum of the first nine numbers, or as 3x8 (a Yin and a Yang number), which is the number of the points of divine light (*jing*) in the body, eight for each of its three stages.

Number 36 allows several deconstructions. The division by 9 and 36 of Heaven and Earth, described in the Shangqing texts, does not correspond to a numerology based on six and three, as has been believed.[67] The 36 Heavens listed in the *Waiguo fangpin* (Distribution of the Outer Realms) actually derive from nine primordial Heavens,

---

[64] *Zhouyi cantong qi*, 1.19a.

[65] *Taishang Laojun shuo wudou jinzhang shousheng jing*, 3a-5a; *Daofa huiyuan*, 67.3a-b; and *Huangdi yinfu jing zhujie*, 14b-16a.

[66] *Sun zhenren beiji qianjin yaofang*, 1.7b.

[67] Zürcher, "Buddhist Influence on Early Taoism: A Survey of Scriptural Evidence," pp. 126–27.

each of which presides over three other Heavens, giving nine groups of four (3+1) Heavens.[68] This number means therefore 3+1, and with it we are still in the range of the celestial numbers; it does not refer to the four directions of the Earth. Parallel to this arrangement of the 36 Heavens, a different one is found in the Lingbao texts, which is incompatible with it. Here 32 Heavens are arranged horizontally in groups of eight, one for each of the four quadrants. We can see once more that Four and Eight govern the horizontal plane, while Three and Nine pertain to the vertical plane. In contrast, the thirty-six "outer" lands listed in the first chapter of the *Waiguo fangpin* are divided into six groups of six, earthly numbers.[69]

Thirty-six is also the number of the provinces of the Celestial Masters. This number is related to the 360 days of the year, just like Twenty-four is the number of the 24 breaths of the year. The reference here is to temporal divisions rather than the terrestrial or celestial quality of the numbers. Also in the temporal domain, Heaven accomplishes 360 rotations in one year; after 3,600 rotations it completes a "small era," and the Yang is exhausted. Meanwhile, the Earth moves by 330 degrees in one year; after traveling 3,300 degrees, the Yin of a "small era" is exhausted.[70] The number 330 seems to be obtained from the multiplication of 6, the figure of Great Yin, by 55, "the number of Heaven and Earth." According to another view, the cosmos comes to an end every 36 billions or trillions of years, and it is the number 36 that counts.[71]

However, while the 360 joints of the body correspond to the number of days in the year, a thirteenth-century Taoist text, more concerned with making reference to the speculative system derived from the *Yijing*, counts 36 heavens because 36 = 4x9, where 9 is the number of Qian ☰; and 36 earths, because 6x6 is the number of Kun ☷. This number matches the 36 arteries in the head (Heaven) and in the stomach (Earth); by adding these two sets of 36, we obtain 72, the number of periods (*hou*) in one year.[72] The "fundamental number of blood" of menstruation is 36 "bushels" (*dou*), because it is the prod-

---

[68] *Shangqing waiguo fangpin Qingtong neiwen*, chapter 2.

[69] See also *Haiqiong Bai zhenren yulu*, 1.9b.

[70] *Sandong zhunang*, 9.1a. The great cosmic eras are associated with numbers 9,900 for Heaven and 9,300 for the Earth.

[71] *Taishang miaoshi jing*, 1a-b.

[72] *Haiqiong Bai zhenren yulu*, 1.9 b-10a.

uct of six by six.[73] The Grotto-Heavens (*dongtian*), which are earthly paradises, are 36, and the Blissful Lands (*fudi*) are 72: being more earthly, they are multiplied by two, the first Yin number. On the basis of the division of the year into six Yang and six Yin months, 36 as a product of 6x6 (the Yin number), multiplied by 4 for the four seasons, gives 144 (related to the 144 teeth and joints). According to the counting of the alchemists, this is the number of the Yin days in the year, because 144 is the number of Kun, pure Yin, in the *Xici*. On the other hand, the number of the Yang days is 216, which is the number of Qian, pure Yang (related to the 216 tendons).[74] This number should be read as follows: 6x9 (nine, great Yang) x4. The total of Yin and Yang days is 360.[75]

As part of the alchemical speculations inspired by the symbolic numbers of the *Yijing*, one removes the four basic hexagrams—Qian ☰, Kun ☷, Kan ☵, and Li ☲—and counts 360 lines for the remaining sixty hexagrams. The 24 lines of the four removed hexagrams correspond to the 24 breaths of the year. But 360 is also obtained by counting 30 days for 12 hexagrams (one per month), and if one adds 5 for the five agents, one obtains 365, the number of days in one year. Adding the 24 breaths to the 360 days of the year, instead, we obtain 384, which corresponds to the total number of lines in the sixty-four hexagrams.

While, as we have seen, in the tradition of the *Yijing* the "number of Heaven and Earth," 55, is the sum of 30 for the Earth and 25 for Heaven, a text of internal alchemy obtains the same number by adding the "emergent" and the "achieved" numbers of each of the five agents: for Water, 1+6 = 7; for Fire, 2+7 = 9; for Wood, 3+8 = 11; for Metal, 4+9 = 13; and for Soil, 5+10 = 15. The numbers assigned to the five agents total therefore 55. This number "creates and completes the five agents," and the author presents this computation under the title "Chart of the Five Agents" ("Wuxing tu").[76]

[73] *Xishan qunxian huizhen ji*, 3.9b-10a.
[74] *Zhouyi cantong qi zhu*, 3.15a.
[75] Baldrian-Hussein, *Procédés secrets du joyau magique*, p. 127. See also, for example, *Taigu ji*, 3.2a; and *Jindan fu*, 3.1a-b.
[76] *Taigu ji*, 2.8a-b.

INTERNAL ALCHEMY

Numbers are used in internal alchemy mainly to regulate the Fire regime (*huohou*); therefore they are sometimes called the "numbers of fire" (*huoshu*), with reference to the rhythm of the alchemical Work. Since the Fire regime involves time and measurement, it makes it possible to organize the functioning of the two Principles, which should be both joined to and separated from one another.[77] The Fire regime reflects the interaction of these Principles, their dynamism, and the measurable and rhythmic nature of their cyclical movements.

Alchemy claims to seize the secret mechanism of the universe. While the Dao is ineffable and immeasurable, say the alchemists, the highness of Heaven and the lowness of the Earth (space), and the beginning and end of the cycles of Yin and Yang (time), can be measured by means of numbers and calculations in order to understand the principle of spatiotemporal operation. This enables one to "know the great Dao."[78] Knowledge by means of numbers is the "hidden spring" (*xuanji*) of the cosmos.[79] "On a large scale, Heaven and Earth, and on a small scale, the whole body, all possess the emergent and achieved numbers of the Fire regime."[80]

In this context, numbers serve as important reference points. First, they make it possible to accord the rhythm of the bodily energies and the alchemical Work to the rhythm of the universe. In addition, the computations over which numbers preside indicate a concern for the integrity of the body (expressed by numbers that measure the agreement between the "internal" and the "external") and for the "divine breaths" (*shenqi*) of the body.[81] Therefore one is constantly advised to comply with the numbers without error and without excess or shortage. This concern is reflected by the frequent use of such terms as "gather" or "collect" (*ju*), "making full" (*quan*), and "making sufficient" (*manzu*); by the frequent allusion to the idea of limits, of measures that should not be exceeded; and by the no less frequent mention of the clepsydra.

---

[77] While they are typified by the Yin-Yang pair, the two Principles can also be Heaven and Earth, Water and Fire, Lead and Mercury, etc. (see below).

[78] See, for example, *Bichuan Zhengyang zhenren Lingbao bifa*, 1.5b.

[79] *Hunyuan bajing zhenjing*, 4.8b, and other texts.

[80] *Huanzhen ji*, 1.10b, dated 1392.

[81] *Hunyuan bajing zhenjing*, 4.8b.

The texts that insist on the physiological aspect of the alchemical Work are especially those that use quantitative calculations, typically based on symbolic numbers and often used in conjunction with breathing. The Fire regime represents the active and practical side of the alchemical Work, which consists in "activating" Fire (by extending or holding breathing) or in "decreasing" it, depending on the different stages of the alchemical Work. In this regard, the numbers establish an association among the year, the month, and the day, and thus enable one to accelerate the alchemical process. This, however, seems to go beyond the simple method of an "acceleration of time" discussed by Nathan Sivin,[82] and to pertain to the broader context of the miniaturization of the world.

Distances and time

The distance that separates Heaven from Earth is related to time using theories about the rise and fall of Yin and Yang. Performing an entire cycle in one nycthemeron or one year, Yin and Yang accomplish a journey that in most cases is deemed to measure 84,000 *li* (a number borrowed from Buddhism). The Yang rising from the winter solstice to the summer solstice runs for 42,000 *li*, and so does the Yin during the second half of the year. The year is divided into different periods based on number Five: 5 days make one *hou*, which contains 60 hours correlated with the 60 spirits of the celestial and the earthly cyclical signs;[83] three *hou* form one *jie* of 45 days; two *jie* contain 90 days, corresponding to one *qi* or one season; and 72 *hou* make one year. This makes it possible to calculate how many *li* both Yin or Yang rise and descend in one year.

Similarly, the day is divided into hours marked by the earthly cyclical signs. Yang rises from *zi* (23h-1h) to *wu* (11h-13h), after which the growth of Yin begins. As these signs mark both the times of the day and those of the year, one can calculate the ascent and the descent of Yin and Yang in the year and in the nycthemeron. The physiological work of breathing is performed according to the model of the increase and decrease of each of these principles. Their ascent and descent in the human body is calculated by establishing a correspon-

---

[82] Sivin, "The Theoretical Background of Elixir Alchemy," p. 243.
[83] *Hunyuan bajing zhenjing*, 5.9a.

Isabelle Robinet

dence between the viscera and the cardinal points (or the seasons), and therefore the hours of the day. This is the basic principle of the physiological aspect of internal alchemy. To do so, one inspiration is deemed to be equivalent to one advance of the Yin breath (interiorization, contraction), while one expiration is equivalent to one advance of the Yang breath (expansion, externalization). If we take as a basis the 84,000 *li* that separate Heaven from Earth, by virtue of the principle of analogy between microcosm and macrocosm that presides over this way of thinking, the heart (= Heaven) and the kidneys (= Earth) are separated from one another by 8.4 inches. An exact parallel can then be made between the routes of ascent and descent of Yin and Yang in the cosmos and in the human body, taking as a basis the cyclical signs that indicate the hours. By assigning a number to each viscera, according to the subdivision of numbers into "emergent," "mature," and "old" that we have mentioned above, and by linking the viscera to the four cardinal directions and the Center, one regulates the number of revolutions assigned to each viscera, in order to move the breath from one to another viscera in accordance with the annual and the daily times. In this way, one accomplishes a "celestial revolution," which consists in matching the circulation of breath in the body with its circulation in the universe. This is called the "Method of the Numbers and Times of the Breaths of the Birth and Completion of Yin and Yang, the Three Primes, the Four Images, and the Five Agents."[84] One can also divide the day into 100 *ke*, which gives 36,000 *ke* in one year, and then proceed to other speculative calculations related to the movements of the Sun or to the cyclical signs.[85]

Moreover, according to the system of correspondences established since the Han period, the 12 months of the year are related to the hexagrams, the 12 pitch pipes, and the 12 hours of the day. The link between the 64 hexagrams and what is counted by 12 is made through number 6: just like each hexagram has 6 lines, so does the day contain

[84] *Id.*, 4.5b.

[85] In the context of the present essay I cannot provide full details on the relation between the numbers and times of breathing and the distance traveled by cosmic bodies. The reader is referred to the work of Farzeen Baldrian-Hussein, *Procédés secrets du joyau magique*, especially pp. 95–96, and possibly to other texts, including *Jindan zhizhi*, 10a-b; *Jindan sibai zi*, 3a; and *Hunyuan bajing zhenjing*, 5.10a-b, which presents a different system.

68

6 Yin and 6 Yang hours, and so do the pitch pipes consist of 6 "female" and 6 "male" pipes. By multiplying 6x6 (one pipe per month) we obtain 36, which is the "achieved number" of Yin. This concerns the months. If, instead, we multiply those 6 months by 9, the number of Yang, we obtain 54, which is the "achieved number" of Yang. The numbers 6 and 9 are used to show, for example, the ascent and descent of the Sun and Moon in one month.[86]

The 360 days of the year can also be deconstructed as 36 (6 months x 6 Yin) multiplied by 4 = 144, which is the number of Kun (pure Yin); and 54 (9 x 6 months) multiplied by 4 = 216, which is the number of Qian (pure Yang); and 216+144 = 360. This is based on the numbers of Qian and Kun in the *Xici*.[87]

Trigrams and hexagrams

As is well known, trigrams and hexagrams are, with the alchemical images in the strict sense, the main symbols that support internal alchemy. Li Daochun, for example, dealing with the qualities and the times (*shishi*) of the alchemical Work, states that they are witnessed by the examination of the hexagrams.[88]

The numbers are among the tools used to represent the hexagrams, and therefore to connect to one another these emblematic figures that, in their totality, symbolize the cosmos. Number 60 governs the rhythm adopted to regulate the times of breathing in order to form a hexagram, because 36 (6x6) forms one line of Qian, called the "Yang fire," and 24 (6x4) forms one line of Kun, called the "Yin fire" (36+24 = 60). One then should perform this kind of exercise 192 times to obtain the number 384, which is the number of the totality of lines in the *Yijing* (64x6).[89] By doing so, one obtains this

---

[86] Therefore, in addition to the computation based on number 5, there is also a system based on the symbolic numbers of Yin and Yang, 6 and 9, as wells as 7 and 8. Thus, the number of the 72 *hou* that make one year is deemed to be obtained by multiplying 9x8.

[87] *Jindan fu*, 31a-b, which refers expressly to the *Xici*. On this subject see, for example, Baldrian-Hussein, *Procédés secrets du joyau magique*, pp. 133–34. See also *Hunyuan bajing zhenjing*, 4.10a-b and 5.9a-b; and *Taishang huadao dushi xianjing*, 5a-b.

[88] *Zhonghe ji*, 1.10a.

[89] See Baldrian-Hussein, *Procédés secrets du joyau magique*, p. 132, and,

symbolic figure that indicates the cosmic totality and represents "the number of the circulation of the Sun and the Moon, and the spring of the creation of Heaven and Earth."[90] Number 384 is also formed by the multiplication of 24 (the number of the "breaths" of the year) by 16; this constitutes a "celestial revolution."[91] The above-mentioned *Hunyuan bajing zhenjing* also matches the number of the "external" lines to the same number of the "internal" spirits.[92]

By counting the breaths, which form either a Yin or a Yang line, one therefore can represent any desired hexagram. Then one relies on the course of the hexagrams in space and time to establish the rhythm of the alchemical Work.

According to another computation, one removes the four hexagrams that represent the four instruments of the alchemical Work (Qian ☰, the furnace; Kun ☷, the tripod; Li ☲, Fire; and Kan ☵, Water), and retains only 60 hexagrams, which punctuate the rhythm of the Work during the year. In fact, the remaining 60 hexagrams contain a total of 360 (6x60) lines, corresponding to the days of the year. According to one of the relevant methods, then, from the winter to the summer solstice (the time of rising Yang) one works on the 180 Yang lines of the *Yijing* in order to "purify the yellow gold" (Yang). During the second half of the year, which is the time of the growth of Yin, one works on the 180 Yin lines in order to purify "the aqueous silver" (Yin).[93]

Through the hexagrams, a link is established with the hours of the day or the times of the year, because each of these is mapped to the hexagrams. In addition, by choosing twelve hexagrams to represent the sequence going first from the birth of Yang to pure Yang, then from the birth of Yin to pure Yin—in other words, from Fu ䷗ to Qian ☰ and from Gou ䷫ to Kun ☷—one reproduces the cycle, both annual and daily, of the growth and decline of Yin and Yang.

While it is not possible to dwell here on all aspects of this subject, we should add that certain virtues are assigned to certain hexagrams.[94] Moreover, the hexagrams lines are also related to mea-

---

for example, *Shangqing Lingbao dafa*, 2.23b-25b.
[90] *Taishang jiuyao xinyin miaojing*, 4a-b.
[91] *Mei xian guanji*, 4.8a-b.
[92] *Hunyuan bajing zhenjing*, 4.8b and 5.3a-b.
[93] *Shangsheng xiuzhen sanyao*, 8.6a-b.
[94] For the hexagrams Tai ䷊ and Pi ䷋ see Baldrian-Hussein, *Procédés*

sures of length according to different equivalences. This makes it possible to assess the advance of breath and blood along the course that one wants them to take in the body.[95]

Weight measurements: Two and Eight

The Fire regime is also measured in terms of the weight of the ingredients. The units that are most often used are the *liang* (ounce), consisting of 24 *zhu*, and the *jin* (pound), consisting of 16 *liang* and 384 *zhu*.[96] The 64 hexagrams "weigh," therefore, 384 *zhu*.

The term *liang*, however, hides a pun, as this character means both "two" and "ounce." The expressions "Two-Eights" and "two *liang*," which are found in works as fundamental as the *Cantong qi* and the *Wuzhen pian*, and have been extensively glossed, are therefore synonymous. They designate the two opposite/complementary principles that form the basis of alchemy: Lead and Mercury, or Dragon and Tiger. As the alchemists repeatedly say, the whole alchemical Work comes down to these two principles. As it takes 2x8 = 16 *liang* to form one pound, one must join Lead and Mercury weighing 8 *liang* each in order to form the one pound that represents the completion of the Work, the Elixir. As Li Daochun explains, however, it is not truly a matter of weight; the meaning is that the two elements should be taken in equal parts.[97] Chen Zhixu adds that the 8 *liang* correspond to half a pound of essence of the Sun and the Moon (Yin and Yang), respectively.[98] Moreover, 16 *liang*, as we have said, consist of 384 *zhu*. Thus we obtain again the cosmic figure of 384, which summarizes the entire *Yijing*. Furthermore, the Two-Eights are also equivalent to the number of pure Yang, Qian, which is 216 (2x8 = 16).[99]

Finally, when the rhythm of the Work accords with the phases of the Moon and the movements of the Sun, the "two *liang*" designate the cyclical signs *mao* and *you*, emblems of the East and the West, respectively (see table 9). In the year, therefore, the "two *liang*" repre-

---

secrets du joyau magique, p. 96.

[95] Baldrian-Hussein, *id.*, p. 92.

[96] In addition to these, other units are also used. See Baldrian-Hussein, *id.*, p. 91.

[97] *Zhonghe ji*, 3.28a.

[98] *Shangyang zi jindan dayao*, 7.6b.

[99] *Id.*, 7.13a.

sent the spring and autumn equinoxes, when Yin and Yang are equal. In the month, they correspond instead to the time of the half moon, because on the eighth day of the month, the first half moon is in the Heart of Heaven in the *you* hour; and on the twenty-third day, the second half moon is in the Center of Heaven in the *mao* hour.[100] The two phases of the Moon, one rising and one declining, are the two *liang* that "rise" and "descend." Together they correspond to the Two-Eights, whose totality makes the full Moon, a symbol of the achievement of the Work and of the one pound.[101] According to other formulations, the Two-Eights constitute "the golden body of one *zhang* and six" (= 16 feet), and "creation is contained in the stove of the Two-Eights."[102]

The union of the Two-Eights representing the union of the opposite poles is also a symbol of primordial Chaos. By virtue of it, when it is accomplished, the "Breath of the True One," the *materia prima* of the alchemical Work, appears. Having joined the Two, the Saint in One instant obtains the "one grain" (i.e., the one grain of the Elixir), and the Yang Elixir rises like the Sun above the sea.[103] A commentary to the *Wuzhen pian* distinguishes between the External Elixir (here, the cosmic symbols), which stands for the Two-Eights making one pound because two half moons are equivalent to one full moon; and the Internal Elixir, where one should circulate Fire in agreement with the 64 hexagrams. This is also compared to the Two-Eights because the 64 hexagrams total 384 lines, corresponding to the 384 *zhu* contained in one pound.[104]

---

[100] Equinoxes and half moons are crucial times when either Yin or Yang is about to prevail over the other. See, for example, *Shangyang zi jindan dayao*, 7.8b-9b.

[101] *Longhu huandan juesong*, 5b (tenth century). As is said in the *Cantong qi*, "The rising half moon corresponds to the trigram Dui ☱ (South-East in the arrangement "prior to Heaven"), and the waning half moon to Gen ☶ (North-West); they make two weights of eight *liang*, which join their essences and form Qian and Kun; Two-Eight corresponds to one pound." *Zhouyi cantong qi*, 1.15a.

[102] *Shangyang zi jindan dayao*, 16.2a and 5.5a.

[103] *Ziyang zhenren wuzhen pian zhushu*, 3.5a-6a.

[104] *Id.*, 3.8b-9a.

CONCLUSION

Nevertheless, it is essential to remember that the alchemists repeat with insistence that numbers are only metaphors. We have "established symbols" so that we may reduce one year to one month, one month to one day, one day to one hour, and the Work to one breath, says for example the *Huanzhen ji* (Anthology of Reverting to Reality), reminding also that Zhang Boduan stated that "one should not divide time into *zi* and *wu*, or establish Qian and Kun into lines and hexagrams."[105] Zhang Boduan himself says that "the Fire regime does not have time" and that "*mao* and *you* are only empty similitudes (*xubi*)."[106] For the *Jindan zhizhi* (Straightforward Directions on the Golden Elixir), if one wants to take hold of the figure of 36,000 (the number of *ke* in the year), one should "place one's hand on the spring of the axis of Yin and Yang, and seize the creative activity of Heaven and Earth: this corresponds to [the time of] a single thought in man."[107]

This way of rectifying falls within the general framework of a warning that the alchemists repeat many times against those who take their statements at face value. It reflects a certain subitist character of the alchemical Work, recurrent and eternal, and the paradoxical nature of internal alchemy that both constructs and deconstructs, and seeks to join the One and the Many.[108] In addition, this way of speaking reminds us that we are dealing with a "living time" that escapes any defined chronological sequence, and in which beginning and end are either interchangeable or confused. In fact, the texts that provide all sorts of details about the time of the Fire regime also say that the rhythm of that regime remains secret and is never disclosed by the masters, if not by word of mouth, or from heart to heart.

The alchemists, thus, highlight the limits of the function of numbers, marked not only by what is unmeasurable, the infinite, but also by the infinitesimal nuances of change and movement.

---

[105] *Huanzhen ji*, 1.10b-11a.
[106] *Jindan sibai zi*, 9a.
[107] *Jindan zhizhi*, 10a-b.
[108] See Robinet, *Introduction à l'alchimie intérieure taoïste*.

On the Meaning of the Terms
Waidan and *Neidan*

INTRODUCTION

Chinese bibliographers and modern historians of Taoism commonly use the term *neidan* (Internal Elixir) in contrast with *waidan* (External Elixir). While *waidan* refers to laboratory alchemy, *neidan* designates a new discipline that appears within Taoism from the eighth century (from this time, at least, we have its first written traces).

One reason for using the term *neidan* can be found in the earliest texts, such as the one by Tao Zhi (?–826), that emphatically distinguish themselves from laboratory alchemy, repeating with insistence that their Work is not concerned with "external things" (*waiwu*).[1] Another justification is provided by the *Yunji qiqian* (Seven Lots from the Bookbag of the Clouds), a major anthology of Taoist texts that presents the works of this discipline under the rubric of Neidan. In the *Yunji qiqian*, however, the works concerned with "chemical" alchemy are not classified under the heading of Waidan, but of Jindan (Golden Elixir). In fact, the term *neidan* is used in an entirely different way in the texts of this discipline, where the discipline itself is typically designated as *jindan* (Golden Elixir), *dadan* (Great Elixir), or *jinye huandan* (Golden Liquor and Cyclical Elixir).[2]

---

[1] *Huanjin shu*, 5a.

[2] I translate *huandan* as "cyclical elixir" instead of "transmuted elixir," as is often done, on account of a fundamental idea frequently expressed in the texts—namely, the perpetual cyclical movement and the principle of circularity and transitivity in both directions: Water generates Metal that generates Water. See, for example, *Zhouyi cantong qi fenzhang tong zhenyi*, 2.23a. We observe very often the pattern "A generates B that generates A": for example, Non-being generates Being that returns to Non-being; or, Cinnabar generates Metal that returns to Cinnabar. See *Longhu huandan jue*, 1.4a, 1.6a.

Isabelle Robinet

To avoid confusion, I will use in this essay the term "internal alchemy" to describe the discipline itself, and the term *neidan* (Internal Elixir, in contrast with *waidan*, External Elixir) to designate the object of my discussion.

Chen Guofu appears to have been the first scholar who tried to trace the contours of internal alchemy.[3] According to Joseph Needham, the term *neidan* appears for the first time in the sixth century under the brush of the Buddhist monk Huisi. *Neidan* refers at that time to physiological alchemy, but the relevant source may contain an interpolation.[4] Farzeen Baldrian-Hussein provides further evidence of this use, possibly dating from the fifth century but based on later secondary sources. She concludes by suggesting that while the term *neidan* may have been used earlier, it became current only during the Song period.[5] This is quite reasonable, as it was at that time that internal alchemy became widespread and truly aware of its uniqueness.

Except for this, we have no explanation of the meaning of the term *neidan* in the earliest stages of its use. The study by Baldrian-Hussein provides information on the terms *neidan* and *waidan*, *waiyao* and *neiyao* (External and Internal Medicine), *yindan* and *yangdan* (Yin and Yang Elixir), and *dadan* and *dayao* (Great Elixir and Great Medicine). The author, however, does not truly pronounces herself on their meanings, since her study, as suggested by its title, is mainly concerned with the "origin and use" of those terms. The passages devoted by Needham to this subject are based on few and fragmentary texts, and his conclusions are at times somewhat hasty.

Without pretending to be comprehensive, I will try to clarify this issue. In different times and according to different authors, the terms *neidan* and *waidan* take on different shades of meaning, and are indeed confusing. Both terms, moreover, were used within both laboratory alchemy and internal alchemy.[6] I propose to throw some light on these different meanings, limiting myself to the texts of internal alchemy.

[3] Chen Guofu, *Daozang yuanliu kao*, pp. 438–53.
[4] Needham, *Science and Civilisation in China*, vol. V, pt. 5, p. 140.
[5] See Baldrian-Hussein, "Inner Alchemy: Notes on the Origin and Use of the Term *Neidan*."
[6] See Baldrian-Hussein, *id.*, p. 179.

76

The question is not simple, and has been further complicated by some Taoist scholars. Li Yuanguo, for instance, relates it to the sexual practices.[7] In his view, the External Medicine (*waiyao*) would be gathered by a man from a woman during sexual intercourse. Li Yuanguo bases himself on the commentaries to the *Wuzhen pian* (Awakening to Reality) by Weng Baoguang and by Chen Zhixu (also known as Shangyang zi), respectively dating from the twelfth and the fourteenth centuries.[8] Li Yuanguo's interpretation is unwarranted: as we shall presently see, those authors give quite different explanations. More importantly, the remarks made by those authors against the sexual practices are as much deprecatory as those of other authors whom Li Yuanguo ranks among the opponents of sexual practices, exactly on the basis of those remarks.

In particular, Weng Baoguang clearly explains in his commentary to the *Wuzhen pian* that those who, in order to translate the *neidan* in terms of sexual practices, base themselves on the argument of the infertility of pure Yin and Yang (an argument relied on by Li Yuanguo as well, but which is present everywhere, beginning with the *Cantong*

---

[7] See Li Yuanguo, *Daojiao qigong yangshengxue*. The issue of sexual practices in Neidan is complicated by the fact that while these practices probably existed, this does not mean that the masters recommended them. Joseph Needham's positivist spirit pushes him too often to regrettable misunderstandings, analogous to his claim that a text such as the *Huangqi yangjing jing* (Scripture of the Yellow Breath and the Yang Essence) teaches the practice of "heliotherapy," while it deals with meditations on the Sun *and the Moon* that can be performed in the shade of a room. It is a true contradiction when, in his *Science and Civilisation in China*, vol. V, part 5, p. 212, Needham translates for the purposes of his "sexual" thesis: "As for disclosing [the nature of] the lead in the reaction-vessel, if you wish to judge of it, it is necessary to fix the Yang fire so that it plays underneath, but it must not be allowed to spread so that it attains the intensity of human passion. This is to show the practitioner under instruction where he must stop. This decision is called the Mysterious Axis." Having said earlier that the woman's body is the "reaction-vessel" and the man's body is the stove, Needham adds that fire is "of course the masculine ardour," and that the text deals with *coitus interruptus*. However, the passage simply states: "You must learn the precise rules governing the Tripod and the Lead, so that the Yang fire may descend and spread. If you do not meet a perfect man who gives you teachings, how can you discover the Mysterious Axis?" See *Jinye huandan yinzheng tu*, 3b.

[8] Li Yuanguo, *Daojiao qigong yangshengxue*, p. 412, quoting, without references, *Ziyang zhenren wuzhen pian zhushu*, 7.2a-b, and *Ziyang zhenren wuzhen pian sanzhu*, 1.10b.

qi) have not understood, because "man" and "woman" are not meant literally and should be intended as metaphoric terms.[9] The same says Chen Zhixu in his *Jindan dayao* (Great Essentials of the Golden Elixir).[10] On the other hand, sexual metaphors are also used by such authors as Chen Nan, ranked by Li Yuanguo among the supporters of the "pure practice," which excludes sexual practices.[11] One wonders on what grounds can one use the same argument first in one direction and then in the opposite direction, consider the denials of some authors and not those of others, and decide that some authors use metaphors while others should be understood literally. In fact, Li Yuanguo is aware of the fragility of his argument: he quotes Weng Baoguang's remarks against the sexual practices, but immediately deprives them of authority with no other argument than his own personal interpretation.[12]

Reverting to our subject, that interpretation is partly based on the terms *waidan* and *neidan*, which Li Yuanguo relates, as do the authors of alchemical texts, to the terms *bi* ("the other") and *wo* ("me"). These terms, which are deemed to be parallel—*bi* refers to the *waidan*, and *wo* to the *neidan*—are used in the *Wuzhen pian*. According to Li Yuanguo, *bi* means "she," i.e., the woman from whom one should receive the External Elixir. A more careful reading of the texts will help us to understand what these terms refer to.

I will divide this essay into three parts, unequal in size but organized around the semantic content of the terms *neidan* and *waidan*. In the first part, I rely on several documents that illustrate the diversity of meanings, sometimes contradictory, taken on by these terms. The second part is devoted to the meanings attributed to these terms by several authors grouped, for convenience, around Chen Zhixu (1290– ca. 1368), as he is the one who appears to be the most explicit. These authors also include Weng Baoguang (fl. 1173), Yu Yan (1258–1314), Li Daochun (fl. ca. 1290), and Zhao Yizhen (late fourteenth century).

---

[9] *Ziyang zhenren wuzhen pian zhushu*, 1.10b and 2.1b. In contrast, Ye Wenshu (also known as Ye Shibiao) seems to have interpreted the *Wuzhen pian* in terms of sexual practices, precisely what Weng Baoguang opposed vigorously. See *Xiuzhen shishu*, 27.3a.

[10] *Shangyang zi jindan dayao*, 5.13a and 3.3b.

[11] *Zhixuan pian* (Pointing to the Mystery), in *Xiuzhen shishu*, 3.3b. See Li Yuanguo, *Daojiao qigong yangshengxue*, p. 399.

[12] Li Yuanguo, *Daojiao qigong yangshengxue*, p. 414.

Some of them are quoted by Chen Zhixu, who shares their views. It should be noted that they include authors whom Li Yuanguo claims to be supporters of sexual practices, as well as authors whom he deems to support the "pure practice." The third and last part is devoted to further explanations given by some of these authors on the distinctions and interactions between the "external" and the "internal."

I. DIVERSITY OF MEANINGS

To illustrate the variety of meanings given to the terms *neidan* and *waidan*, we shall begin by comparing two texts that in this regard are opposite to one another.

1. The *Taishang jiuyao xinyin miaojing* (Most High Wondrous Scripture of the Mind Seal and Its Nine Essentials) briefly states that the *neidan* concerns the true Breath, in contrast to the *waidan* that concerns the breath of food, i.e., the ordinary and coarse human breath.[13] This view is similar to the one of Qiu Chuji (1146–1227), for whom the true breath of original Yang is hidden inside, while the external concerns the (spermatic?) essence (*jing*) and blood, i.e., physiology.[14]

2. The *Xuanzong zhizhi wanfa tonggui* (Reintegrating the Ten Thousand Dharmas: A Straightforward Explanation of the Taoist Tradition) explains, instead, that the *neidan* concerns the personal vital breath, and the *waidan* concerns the primordial cosmic Breath. These two breaths are inseparable from one another; the terms *nei* ("internal") and *wai* ("external") have been used to teach that one should "know this (*ci*) and understand that (*bi*)." It is an error, adds this text, to have thought that "external" designates minerals and plants.[15] Here, unlike the previous text, *waidan* refers to what pertains to the primordial Breath. Moreover, we find again the terms *bi* ("that," "the other") to designate the "external," and *ci* or *wo* ("this" or "me") to designate the "internal," on which Li Yuanguo bases his interpretation discussed above. As we can see, here *bi* very clearly designates the cosmic Breath.

---

[13] *Taishang jiuyao xinyin miaojing*, 6a.
[14] *Dadan zhizhi*, 1.1b.
[15] *Xuanzong zhizhi wanfa tonggui*, 3.13b.

Isabelle Robinet

For the other texts that we shall present, *nei* designates the physiological techniques.

3. We should first discuss the *Chen xiansheng neidan jue* (Instructions on the Internal Elixir by Master Chen), attributed to Chen Pu and dating from the late Tang or the early Five Dynasties (ca. tenth century, with a preface dated to the eleventh century).[16] This text exhibits hardly any of the typical features of internal alchemy: it rarely refers to trigrams and hexagrams, and contains few examples of the vocabulary of this discipline. However, it mentions one of the dominant and most representative principles of internal alchemy: True Yin and True Yang are extracted from their opposite principles (here the Sun and the Moon).[17] The text provides a good example of a type of internal alchemy that is not yet very pronounced and is closely related to the methods of Shangqing Taoism, which in some respects constitute—as Michael Strickmann and myself have shown—an "astral alchemy."[18]

In this text, *nei* designates the traditional physiological practices, and *wai* designates the "astral" meditation practices of Shangqing. The astral emanations are the external cosmic elements that allow one to "capture [the mechanism of] universal creation" (*zaohua*), one of the fundamental goals of internal alchemy and one of the formulations that its followers are most fond of. The asterisms provide the external Yin and Yang that are essential to the sublimation of the body, which the text emphasizes and on which it provides details.[19]

This text is different from those examined below in that the "external" concerns only the asterisms. For those that we shall

[16] A variant version of this work is found in *Xiuzhen shishu*, 17.1b ff. The commentary is different, but the "oral instructions" are by Chen Pu. This version erroneously attributes the appellation Niwan xiansheng (Master of the Muddy Pellet), which belongs to Chen Nan (?–1212), to Chen Pu. It also erroneously refers to Chen Pu's work as *Cuixu pian* (The Emerald Emptiness), which is the title of a work by Chen Nan. In other words, the *Xiuzhen shishu* makes confusion between Chen Nan and Chen Pu, to the detriment of the latter who is the actual author of the text discussed here.

[17] *Chen xiansheng neidan jue*, 22a-b.

[18] Strickmann, "On the Alchemy of T'ao Hung-ching," pp. 169–78; Robinet, *La révélation du Shangqing dans l'histoire du taoïsme*, pp. 176–80.

[19] *Chen xiansheng neidan jue*, 10a-b and 17b, respectively.

80

presently approach, *wai* does have a cosmic scope, but in a way that is both broader and more characteristic of internal alchemy. We shall be mainly concerned with four texts: the *Shangdong xindan jingjue* (Instructions on the Scripture of the Heart Elixir of the Highest Cavern); the *Zhigui ji* (Anthology Pointing to Where One Belongs), by Wu Wu (preface dated 1165); the *Waidan neidan lun* (Treatise on the External and the Internal Elixirs), by Yanluo zi; and again the *Xuanzong zhizhi wanfa tonggui* (Reintegrating the Ten Thousand Dharmas: A Straightforward Explanation of the Taoist Tradition). The precise dates of these texts are uncertain, but they seem to have been composed between the late Tang and the early Song periods (ca. ninth/tenth centuries), except for the last one, which dates at least from the twelfth century, and for Wu Wu's work.

For these texts, as we shall see, *wai* or "external" refers to what we call internal alchemy, with all its cosmic and symbolic references; this is in contrast with *nei* or "internal," which designates the ancient physiological practices. *Wai*, in other words, is understood as meaning *waixiang*, or "external symbols," which can either be cosmic or pertain to mineral alchemy. The term *waidan*, says Wang Dao's preface (dated 1185) to the *Longhu jing* (Scripture of the Dragon and the Tiger), does not mean minerals, but cosmic symbols, namely "the essence of Heaven and Earth and the efflorescence of the Sun and the Moon." Wang Dao adds that the basic principle of this alchemy is to "generate matter from non-matter."[20] This is a recurrent theme among the alchemists, who also often say that existence (*you*) arises from non-existence (*wu*).

4. According the *Shangdong xindan jingjue*, one should interiorly practice the *yindan*, or Yin Elixir, which consists in "guarding the Three-One and the Nine chambers."[21] This is obviously a practice of visualization of the bodily spirits in the Cinnabar Fields, similar to the Shangqing practices. These practices only grant longevity and health. "Externally," in contrast, one should take care of the Yang Elixir, which makes it possible to rise to Heaven; this is the Golden Liquor

---

[20] *Guwen longhu jing zhushu*, la.
[21] *Shangdong xindan jingjue*, 2.1b. On this text, see Chen Guofu, *Daozang yuanliu kao*, pp. 309 and 445.

and Cyclical Elixir (*jinye huandan*),[22] a common expression that denotes all of what we call internal alchemy (in particular, it is used by Peng Xiao throughout his commentary to the *Cantong qi*). In fact, the practice of the Yang Elixir is described in a way entirely consistent with the statements on the circulation of breath in internal alchemy, even though almost none of the customary metaphors are used.[23] We may add that according to this text the Internal and External Elixirs "respond to one another" (*xiangying*) and are equally necessary.[24] In this case, therefore, *nei* and *wai* appear to designate the meditation on the bodily spirits and the circulation of breath, respectively.

5. The "external" metaphors or symbols, instead, are involved in the definition of *waidan* given by Yanluo zi and the *Zhigui ji*.

a. For Yanluo zi, the *neidan* concerns the breathing exercises, while the *waidan* involves the Yang Dragon and the Yin Tiger, the liquor of Wood and the essence of Metal.[25]

b. For the *Zhigui ji*, the *neidan* is "nothing but" the heart and the kidneys, and concerns the union of essence and breath, the breathing or the sexual techniques, the ingestion of astral emanations or of herbal drugs, the abstinence from cereals and the observation of chastity, in order to "seek happiness and peace." We have here an enumeration of precisely what the texts of internal alchemy reject as "inferior" or even heterodox practices. The *waidan*, instead, uses Yin and Yang, the trigrams, the "four emblems," the five agents, Lead and Mercury, and the Dragon and the Tiger. The features of the new discipline that is internal alchemy are listed and subsumed under the term *waidan*. Only the *waidan* can confer the status of divine immortal, and it is essential to devote oneself to it after practicing the *neidan*.[26] The text applies a process that is well-known in the history of Taoism, which consists in providing the highest efficacy to the new methods, relegating the old ones to an inferior rank.[27]

---

[22] *Id.*, 1.2a and 2.1b.
[23] *Id.*, 2.7b-8a.
[24] *Id.*, 2.7b.
[25] *Xiuzhen shishu*, 18.7a.
[26] *Zhigui ji*, preface, 1a-b.
[27] See Robinet, *La révélation du Shangqing*, vol. I, pp. 36-39.

c. An example given by Baldrian-Hussein also pertains to this interpretation: according to the biography of Yin Xi, the *neidan* concerns the techniques of breathing and its circulation in the body, and the meditation on the bodily spirits, in contrast to the *waidan* that deals with the Tiger, the Dragon, and the essences of Wood and Metal.[28] Similarly, the *Xiantian xuanmiao yunü taishang shengmu zichuan xiandao* (The Way of Immortality Transmitted by the Most High Holy Mother, Precelestial Jade Woman of Obscure Mystery) states that the *neidan* concerns the practice of breath, and grants only health and longevity; while the *waidan* deals with "the Yang Dragon and the Yin Tiger, the liquor of Wood and the essence of Metal," and the joining of the "two breaths."[29]

We arrive in this context to the paradox that the term *waidan* designates precisely what historians call Neidan.

6. In the same line is also the *Zhong Lü chuandao ji* (Records of the Transmission of the Dao from Zhongli Quan to Lü Dongbin). Zhongli Quan replies to a question asked by Lü Dongbin on what is the *waidan*. The answer is clear. The *waidan* is the mineral chemistry, which serves as a metaphor of the inner practice (*neishi*). Mercury and Silver are comparable to the Yang Dragon and the Yin Tiger; the fire of the heart to the red of Cinnabar; and the water of the kidneys to the black of Lead.[30]

Then the disciple repeats the words of his master and seeks further explanations. The master explains that Lead and Mercury belong to the "external" domain, and that when one moves to internal domain, it is a matter of the human body. After this, he describes the practices of the circulation of breath and the body fluids.[31]

Later on, returning again on this issue, Zhongli Quan explains that the ancient saints and immortals have used these mineral metaphors to describe inner practices; however, one should not stick to the metamorphoses of inanimate matter, such as lead and mercury,

---

[28] See Baldrian-Hussein, "Inner Alchemy: Notes on the Origin and Use of the Term *Neidan*," p. 172.

[29] *Xiantian xuanmiao yunü taishang shengmu zichuan xiandao*, 5a-b.

[30] *Xiuzhen shishu*, 15.8b. On this text, see Baldrian-Hussein, *Procédés Secrets du Joyau Magique*.

[31] *Id.*, 15.11a.

but to the living matter that is found within oneself.[32] Huang Ziru (fl. 1241), commenting on the *Jindan sibai zi* (Four Hundred Words on the Golden Elixir) by Zhang Boduan, agrees with this view: "Red Cinnabar (*zhusha*) and Mercury (*shuiyin*) are external elements. The divine immortals could not do otherwise than using external medicines as metaphors (*yu*) to talk about the *neidan*."[33]

Further on, however, the *Chuandao ji* provides more explanations. The True Breath of the universe comes from outside and enters within. Outside one seizes the cosmic Breath; inside, the primordial Breath must be activated "in a martial way," in order to clear the Yin within the body.[34] This agrees with the theories of the texts discussed in the second part of the present essay, and clarifies that the meaning of *wai* involves the metaphors that serve to give a cosmic dimension to the alchemical Work. This is also how we should understand Wang Dao's preface quoted above,[35] which states that the *neidan* has "the mind and breath as foundations, and the *waidan* has Lead and Mercury as ancestors," since this text, as we have seen, has established that the *waidan* does not deal with minerals, but with cosmic essences.

The meaning given to the terms *nei* and *wai* in these texts clarifies that here it is the *waidan* that grants ascension to Heaven, and not the *neidan*. Needham notes a contradiction between the *Xiuzhen bijue* (Secret Instructions on the Cultivation of Reality; same text, with variants, as the *Waidan neidan lun* by Yanluo zi cited above), of which he provides a quotation, and the *Jindan dayao* (Great Essentials of the Golden Elixir) of Chen Zhixu.[36] According to the first text, the *waidan* concerns the Yin and Yang cosmic breaths, and grants only longevity and health, while the *neidan* pertains to the physiological practices and leads to the ascension to Heaven. The *Jindan dayao* states the opposite.[37] We shall now examine the perspective of this text and those that share its views, which will enable us to understand this difference.

[32] *Id.*, 15.18a.
[33] *Id.*, 5.6b.
[34] *Id.*, 16.8a-b.
[35] *Guwen longhu jing zhushu*, 1b-2a.
[36] Needham, *Science and Civilisation in China*, vol. V, part 5, p. 37.
[37] *Id.*, pp. 40–44.

II. *NEIDAN* AND *WAIDAN*, YIN AND YANG,
XIANTIAN AND *HOUTIAN*

Chen Zhixu, also known as Shangyang zi, will serve initially as a reference point for a more advanced understanding of the terms *waidan* and *neidan*, because of the many elucidations that he provides on this point. I will rely on his *Jindan dayao* and on his commentary to the *Wuzhen pian*.[38] Chen Zhixu often quotes in this connection Weng Baoguang and Li Daochun, implying that he shares the understanding of these two authors.

1. External: Polar cosmic principles — Internal: Purification and assimilation of those principles

The breath in question, says Chen Zhixu, is not the breath of respiration, but the "external" breath, which is the Black Lead and pertains to the alchemical way (*jindan*). It is the same as what Buddhists call the Dharma (*fa*), and Confucians the sentiments of humanity and righteousness (*ren* and *yi*). This breath is used in the Great Vehicle of the three teachings, and is indispensable to attain Buddhahood or immortality. It is contrasted to the "internal" breath, which is the Black Mercury and pertains to the practice of concentration (*xiuding*) and to the natural Dao. It is the median harmony (*zhonghe*) of the Confucians and the *shiyin* (probably meaning Guanshiyin, or Guanyin) of the Buddhists. This is the Way that the great saint should practice in his teaching.[39]

Therefore the "external" breath pertains to the ultimate Truth, and the "internal" breath to its actuation. The external Breath is the

[38] *Shangyang zi jindan dayao*; *Ziyang zhenren wuzhen pian zhushu*; and *Ziyang zhenren wuzhen pian sanzhu*. Chen Zhixu's commentary to the *Wuzhen pian* is found in the *Sanzhu*, after the commentaries by Lu Ziye and Weng Baoguang. Weng Baoguang's commentary is erroneously attributed to Xue Daoguang, but the works of these two authors contain some shared portions. Xue Daoguang's commentary, which is almost entirely lost except for the passages inserted into Weng Baoguang's commentary, appears to be the first commentary of the *Wuzhen pian*: see *Ziyang zhenren wuzhen pian zhushu*, 1.2b-5b and 6a, where Weng Baoguang cites a *benzhu* ("original commentary") which is the one by Xue Daoguang, and corresponds to *Ziyang zhenren wuzhen pian sanzhu*, 1.1a-b and 3a-b.
[39] *Shangyang zi jindan dayao*, 2.2a.

Isabelle Robinet

particle of Breath of the True Yang possessed by all human beings. It comes from outside, and in the alchemical Work it is the "master" or the "host" (zhu), because what comes from outside is the master and what is inside is the guest, according to the principle of inversion (diandao) that presides over the entire alchemical way.[40] This Breath is symbolized by Qian ☰ and Kun ☷, and by Li ☲ and Kan ☵ repositioned at the center (li-ji and kan-wu). On the contrary, the Essence of Metal (jinjing) and the Liquor of Wood (muye), Red Lead and Black Mercury pertain to the inner domain.[41]

Externally, thus, we have the vertical and horizontal polar cosmic principles (Qian and Kun, Li and Kan) and the Center; internally we have the materials of the alchemical Work already worked upon: Lead is red instead of black, and Mercury is not red as it was at the beginning of the Work, but is black. A transformation and an exchange of attributes has occurred.

2. Internal: Yang within Yin — External: Yin within Yang

According to another system of reference and another formulation, also by Chen Zhixu, the External Medicine (waiyao) is the "Water of the True One prior to Heaven," which is found within the trigram Kan ☵. From it, one draws the Breath of the Supreme One prior to Heaven, which is the Yang within the Yin and the true Lead, the pure Lead prior to Heaven. In contrast, the Internal Medicine (neiyao) is the "Liquor of the True One prior to Heaven," which is found within the trigram Li ☲. This gives the "perfectly true Mercury," which is the Yin within the Yang.[42] The External Medicine is the External Elixir, or the Yang Elixir, and the Internal Medicine is the Internal Elixir, or the Yin Elixir. The Yang or External Elixir consists in obtaining the Breath prior to Heaven and placing it in the tripod. When this is done, the Yin or Internal Elixir consists of purification and nourishment, two terms that designate the Fire regime (huohou).

Moreover, there are also an "internal tripod" and an "external tripod."[43] The "internal tripod" is the lower Cinnabar Field, which Chen Zhixu situates according to the purest yangsheng tradition. The

[40] Id., 11.8a-b and 6.7a.
[41] Ziyang zhenren wuzhen pian sanzhu, 2.21a.
[42] Id., 7.3b-4a.
[43] Id., 5.6b.

86

"external tripod," he says quoting Weng Baoguang,[44] is also called "external Furnace" or "Yin Furnace," and is the "Furnace in the shape of a reclined Moon" that contains the Yang breath, which is the rising breath of the Tiger (growth of the Yang within the Yin). The fire of the True One prior to Heaven is born and grows within this Furnace. Its counterpart is the "Yang Tripod," which contains the Yin breath and is the "descending Dragon's Breath" (decrease of the Yin within the Yang).[45]

To summarize, the "external" is the Yang within the Yin (the inner Yang line of Kan ☵) that should grow, and the "internal" is the Yin within the Yang (the inner Yin line of Li ☲) that should decrease, both in terms of the ingredients (Lead and Mercury) and of the Furnace and the Tripod. This accords with the principles of the Chinese tradition, in which Yang is expansion and growth, while Yin is contraction and decrease.

3. External: First step of the "collection" — Internal: growth and maturation

In the mode of action and with regard to the division of the alchemical Work into stages, the "external" is the first step, which is the "extraction" or the "collection"; and the "internal" is the second step, which is the Fire regime.[46] Chen Zhixu adds that the External Medicine or External Elixir, which is also the Yang Elixir, is born in one instant in the Furnace (the extraction is often described as having to occur in an instant outside time). The Internal Medicine or Internal Elixir, which is the Yin Elixir, is obtained after one has placed the External Elixir in the tripod, by practicing the Fire regime by means of the True Fire. "Collecting Lead takes only one instant; joining it to Mercury takes ten months." Collecting the Lead prior to Heaven

---

[44] The quotation corresponds to *Ziyang zhenren wuzhen pian zhushu*, 5.22a-b. Another unacknowledged quotation found later in the same text corresponds to *Ziyang zhenren wuzhen pian zhushu*, 4.18b.

[45] On this subject, see *Shangyang zi jindan dayao*, 5.3b-8b, and, by the same author, *Ziyang zhenren wuzhen pian sanzhu*, 2.21a.

[46] As we have seen, the author explains this in *Shangyang zi jindan dayao*, 5.5a-6a.

pertains to action; joining it to the Mercury posterior to Heaven pertains to non-action.[47]

Chen Zhixu also quotes Li Daochun to say that one should start from the external and move to the internal. Only those who have innate knowledge can practice the internal without first purifying the external. In the domain of action, which is the domain of the external, one distinguishes between "substance" and "function."[48] We are in the field of analytical distinctions, of duality; we are in the order, Chen Zhixu clarifies, of the "appearance body" (seshen, rū-pakāya) of Buddhism, the domain of the external and tangible marks of the Work, and of ming, which here corresponds to the vital force. The "internal" domain, where non-action rules, is the domain of the intangible and the informal, which however truly exists. This is the "body of the law" (fashen, dharmakāya) of Buddhism, and the "true nature" (xing). One should therefore begin with action, which is related to existence (you), and with the life force; only then can one give way to non-action, which pertains to the domain of non-being (wu) that is true existence (zhenyou). At the external stage, one obtains only earthly immortality; at the internal stage, one reaches celestial immortality.[49]

In his commentary to the Wuzhen pian, Chen Zhixu also clarifies that the External Medicine is found within the world of forms (se-xiang) and pertains to the breath of the life force (ming). The Internal Medicine, instead, occurs naturally within oneself and never outside oneself; it pertains to the "true nature" (xing) and to the essence (jing).[50]

The view of Lu Ziye, the author of another commentary to the Wuzhen pian, is the same and uses the basic principle of "reversal." The alchemist works on the True Yang contained within Kan ☵ and on the True Yin enclosed within Li ☲; in fact, says Lu Ziye, Kan takes on a Yang appearance, as it is regarded as containing the Yang, and Li for the same reason takes on a Yin appearance. Because of this, the "me" that originally is Li (of a Yang nature) is on the contrary Yin,

[47] Id., 12.13b.

[48] And not "matter and function," as translated by Needham, Science and Civilisation in China, vol. V, part 5, p. 41. The Chinese words are ti and yong.

[49] Shangyang zi jindan dayao, 5.4b, quoting Li Daochun's Zhonghe ji, 2.4a-b.

[50] Ziyang zhenren wuzhen pian zhushu, 7.5a.

and the "other" that is Kan, is Yang. "Me" is equated with "internal"; it was originally Yang, but has lost its Yang and has become Yin. The Yang therefore is projected to the outside; it must be interiorized and reintegrated. It is the "master" (*zhu*) and Lead. The Yin is Mercury, "the guest" (*ke*); but—once again contrary to the ordinary rules—the Yin, which is the guest, takes the initiative and summons the host.[51] Similarly, the values of "above" and "below" are reversed. Li, which appears to be Yang to ordinary people because it is Yang outside, is placed above, so that in actual fact the Yin is above; and conversely, the Yang is below. Thus, the "foreign" Yang is below; one should make it raise, but also interiorize it and appropriate it.[52]

In the thirteenth century, Xiao Yanzhi (fl. 1260) gives us more details on this subject by dividing the Work into two parts: in the first part, the external Yang is sought by the internal Yin, and in the second one, the external Yang joins the internal Yin.[53]

To avoid overcharging this essay, I will not provide further examples, and will only point out that this interpretation continues at least until the seventeenth century with Wu Chongxu (1574–1644).[54]

4. Xiantian and houtian

In his *Jindan dayao*, Chen Zhixu indulges in one of those paradoxes that the alchemists are fond of. He explains that in the state "prior to the world" (*xiantian*) man gives way to desires and lets his "prior breath" escape. The same happened before the world, when Qian ☰ was taken by desire for Kun ☷, and as a consequence suffered a break and became Li ☲. Similarly, Kun was taken by desire for Qian and gave birth to Kan ☵.[55] Here, in other words, the term *xiantian* refers to the advent of the world of desire.

On the other hand, the Breath prior to Heaven has a dual nature: "It is inside but comes from the outside."[56] Indeed, it is internal as innate and eternal, but comes from the outside as it was exteriorized.

---

[51] See *Xiuzhen shishu*, 9.11b-12a, by Xiao Yanzhi; and Yu Yan's commentary to the *Cantong qi*, *Zhouyi cantong qi fahui*, 5.8b.

[52] *Ziyang zhenren wuzhen pian sanzhu*, 1.13a.

[53] *Xiuzhen shishu*, 9.11b-12a.

[54] *Daozang jiyao*, 1, 7, pp. 54–55.

[55] *Shangyang zi jindan dayao*, 11.8a-b.

[56] *Id.*, 5.3b, and *Ziyang zhenren wuzhen pian sanzhu*, 2.21a.

Thus we can understand why the order of *xiantian* pertains to the practice and the purifying action. On the contrary, in this context, the term *houtian*, "posterior to heaven," refers to the path of "non-action" performed by the practitioner—an action that is non-action—when he encounters a perfect man who teaches him how to join his own breath of True Yang to the cosmic breath. This allows him to become invulnerable, "breathe through the heels," and become celestial.

In other words, at the "external" stage the practitioner must find the state prior to Heaven, which is the state of absolute quietude, where nothing exists yet. This state corresponds to the Great Yin; but it is a silence that gives rise to Yang and to the world, and preludes to the desire to create. The adept, so to speak, becomes Kun ☷, which draws the Yang of Qian ☰ and gives rise to Kan ☵. Thus the adept obtains a Yang line that produces Kan ☵, and then Kan ☵ replaces Kun ☷. This results in the arrangement posterior to Heaven.

As is said in a commentary on a poem by Bai Yuchan, although one "borrows the [term] External Medicine, this has nothing to do with gold or silver, and with plants or material things: it is only the One Breath prior to Heaven and to the division of the *Taiji* (Great Ultimate)."[57] Here, in a text dating from the year 988, we find an explanation of the use of the term *waidan*, pointed out by Farzeen Baldrian-Hussein in her article mentioned above. In this text, in fact, the External Elixir consists in "understanding the meaning of darkness and obscurity." The term translated as "darkness and obscurity" is *huanghu*; it derives from a sentence in *Daode jing* 21 that describes the Dao as something "vague and indistinct" (*hu xi huang xi*), dark and obscure (*youming*), that contains a "thing" (*wu*), an "essence" (*jing*). This passage of the *Daode jing* is constantly quoted in the alchemical texts with regard to the primordial Essence found within the primordial Water, from which the adept draws the original Breath, or the Yang. It is the Yin containing True Yang, the Great Yin that, having reached its extreme, generates the Yang. The Great Yin, or Taiyin, is Kun, but in the texts it is often confused with, superimposed on, or equated to Kan, which contains a Yang line, the rising

---

[57] *Sanji zhiming quanti*, 14b.

Yang.[58] The arrangements prior and posterior to Heaven coincide with one another.

Similarly, Yu Yan distinguishes between two stages: the "emergence" (*chan*), which is the stage prior to Heaven, and the "work" (*gongfu*), which is posterior to Heaven.[59] In the first stage, one "congeals one's spirit and lets it enter into the navel of Kun" (*ning shen ru yu kan qi*). In the second stage, one "carries one's spirit" (*yishen*) to let it rise to the top of Qian.[60]

According to Dai Qizong's (fl. 1332–37) sub-commentary to the *Wuzhen pian*, the External Medicine, which again corresponds to the "emergence," is produced within the Breath prior to Heaven of Kun (*kun xiantian qi*), and thus in the South-West, where the Moon is born. For the alchemists, this is a dual symbol of both Yin and Yang in their state of reflection.[61] "Man is like the Moon, which can be reborn only by receiving the Yang of the Sun," says Chen Zhixu.[62] This medicine is the external Yang. The "seed," adds Dai Qizong, "is in the Internal Medicine of the Breath posterior to Heaven of Qian (*qian houtian qi*), that is, the North-West, in the Northern Sea." This is the Yang born in the Cinnabar Field, in the lower part of the body.

The second stage of the Work is Yin, as it is devoted to internalize and mature, by means the Fire regime, the Yang that purifies the Yin of the human being. As for the important question that remains to be discussed, namely the priority given to the work on one's *ming* (life force) over one's *xing* (inner nature) according to the different "schools," this will be the subject of a separate study.[63] For the moment, let it be enough to say that in the texts examined here, the cultivation of *ming* precedes the cultivation of *xing*, except for the very talented person who is provided with innate knowledge. But this should be qualified, as we shall do in the next section of this essay.

---

[58] See, for example, *Zhonghe ji*, 3.26a.
[59] *Zhouyi cantong qi fahui*, 4.8b.
[60] *Id.*, 5.3b.
[61] *Ziyang zhenren wuzhen pian zhushu*, 3.13b.
[62] *Shangyang zi jindan dayao*, 7.5a-b.
[63] [See Robinet, *Introduction à l'alchimie intérieure taoïste*, chapter VII: "La notion de *xing*." — Ed.]

Weng Baoguang divides Peng Xiao's treatise, the *Jin yuechi* (Golden Key), into two parts.[64] The first one concerns the state "prior to Heaven" and the *waidan*; it deals with "the Black Lead and the aqueous Tiger," and teaches how to capture "the essence of the True One" issued from Water. The second part deals with the personal breath "posterior to Heaven," "the Red Lead and the fiery Dragon," and is concerned with the Fire regime (*huohou*). According to this author, all the ingredients that man can find within himself are "posterior to Heaven" and are Yin in nature; therefore it is necessary to make use of the external Yang.[65] The Essence of the true One is outside; it is the Golden Elixir (*jindan*) and the True Soil (*zhentu*). One should absorb it in one's abdomen, and then it is called True Lead or Yang Elixir; it is the Tiger. Weng Baoguang then describes the course of this Medicine in a traditional way, in accordance with the practices of the circulation of breath. In contrast, one's own true Breath is the Dragon, which rises as a result of the "external" breath that ignites it. Then one should purify one's own Yin Mercury with the Cinnabar "prior to Heaven."

While it takes only one instant to realize the External Medicine, ten months are required to obtain the Golden Liquor and the Cyclical Elixir (*jinye huandan*). The External Medicine is the mother, because it is under its action that the Internal Medicine, its daughter, is born.[66]

> Collecting the Breath prior to Heaven, the True Yin and the True Yang, the Two-Eights (a name of the two principles that are necessary for the Work) of the same nature, seizing them in one instant, purifying and obtaining a particle of supreme Yang Elixir called True Lead: all of this work is external, therefore it is called External Medicine. Projecting (*dian*) the Yang Elixir onto one's own Yin Mercury ... this work is internal, therefore it is called Internal Medicine.[67]

[64] *Ziyang zhenren wuzhen pian zhushu*, 2.15a-b.
[65] Similarly, for the *Jindan zhengzong*, 1b, and the *Shangyang zi jindan dayao*, 3.3b-4a, the *xiantian* is Yang and the *houtian* is Yin. According to Yu Yan (*Zhouyi cantong qi fahui*, 5.8a), the entire human body is Yin, and the Yang is external.
[66] *Ziyang zhenren wuzhen pian zhushu*, 2.14b-15b, 3.6b, 8b, 15a, 17a, and 7.1a-3b.
[67] Id., 7.3b.

On the other hand, Weng Baoguang also ranks as *wai* everything related to the metaphors of internal alchemy, and as *nei* everything corresponding to the inner work; but he uses the same symbols. The External Medicines are the black Lead and the True Mercury, which are the true Breath beginning to move from the Tiger and the Dragon, whose increase and decrease are symbolized by those of the Moon. The Internal Medicines are the Golden Elixir and the true Breath of "myself," and the application of their increase and decrease, the absorption of the White Tiger in the abdomen of the adept where it joins his own Mercury (which is Yin). *Wai* therefore means the cosmological aspect of the physiological work, both of which are expressed in symbolic terms.

To summarize, we can establish these equations: "External" means the Yang within the Yin (as it is not present in man, who is only Yin), the Yang Elixir and the first step of extraction, which is the work on the *ming*. "Internal" means the Yin within the Yang, the Yin Elixir, the second step of "feeding," the work on the *xing*, and the Fire regime.

Man and the world in which we live—as Peng Xiao also says, for example—are entirely Yin, and the Yang therefore is external. It should be integrated. The phase of integration is called "internal," which is logical, and Yin Elixir, because it consists in working on the human Yin by "heating" the Yang that lodges in man. An equation that is frequent in the texts and that we have briefly mentioned earlier is made between the Great Yin, or the trigram Kun ☷, and the Yang within the Yin, or Kan ☵. This makes it possible to say both that man is pure Yin and that he contains Yang.

We come here to one of the paradoxes deliberately used by the alchemists, which challenge our logic. Briefly, these elliptic processes involve establishing an equivalence between what generates and what is generated, the container and the contained. Once again, this consists in superimposing the arrangements of the trigrams prior to Heaven and posterior to Heaven onto one another, so that Kun and Kan are in the same place, with the result that the Great Yin is also the emerging Yang.

Isabelle Robinet

III. INTERRELATION AND INTERACTION
OF INTERNAL AND EXTERNAL

As is always the case in the texts of internal alchemy, the concepts are both well distinguished and handled in such a way that they are intertwined and entangled. The concepts of *nei* and *wai* are no exceptions: "The method establishes the Furnace and the Tripod inside, and yet they are outside. It establishes [the symbols] Kan, Li, Lead, and Mercury outside, and yet they are inside. This is the meaning of the Internal and the External Elixirs," says Weng Baoguang quoting the *Yimen pomi ge* (Yimen's Song on Overcoming Delusion).[68]

To begin, many authors say that the distinction between *nei* and *wai* is "provisional," and belongs only to the laborious domains of the small and the medium vehicles. "The Internal and the External Medicines are only one Dao," states Weng Baoguang.[69] The great vehicle entirely ignores these distinctions.[70] Another master similarly says:

> The Internal Elixir is the personal primordial Breath; the External Elixir is the cosmic primordial Breath. But there is neither an Internal Elixir nor an External Elixir. The personal primordial Breath is the cosmic primordial Breath, and the cosmic primordial Breath is the personal primordial Breath. The Internal and the External cannot be separated even for one instant; if they are separated, this is not the Way. The ancient immortals, fearing that the common people would only understand the Internal Medicine and would not understand the Great Way, have forced themselves to use the words "internal" and "external."[71]

At the same time, we can also modify and multiply the division between "external" and "internal," as does Weng Baoguang.[72] The whole dialectic of the One and the many, which is the very subject of

[68] *Ziyang zhenren wuzhen pian zhushu*, 7.1b.
[69] *Id.*, 7.2a.
[70] *Zhonghe ji*, 2.5b. See also, for example, *Ziyang zhenren wuzhen pian jiangyi*, 4.5a.
[71] Mu Changzhao, *Xuanzong zhizhi wanfa tonggui*, 3.13b.
[72] *Ziyang zhenren wuzhen pian sanzhu*, 2.6a-b.

the alchemical language, is at work here. Both need to be played at the same time.

In his commentary on the *Wuzhen pian*, Weng Baoguang transforms the Internal and the External Medicines into a division that applies at several levels. Thus, "the *po* (Yin) soul of the Earth" is the White Tiger as the External Medicine, and is the Golden Elixir (*jindan*) as the Internal Medicine. "The *hun* (Yang) soul of Heaven" is the Green Dragon in terms of the External Medicine, and is one's own true Essence as the Internal Medicine. The Red Mercury is the descending breath of the Dragon externally, and is one's own true Breath internally. The Metal of the Water (*shuijin*, Metal issued from Water, i.e., the Yang extracted from Water-Yin) is the rising Breath of the Tiger externally, and is the Golden Elixir internally. In other words, "external" refers to terms that use the images of the Tiger and the Dragon, and "internal" refers to terms that involve the "breath" and the "essence." We encounter again what we found at the beginning of this essay: "internal" stands for the physiological practices, and "external" designates the metaphors that are specific to the language of internal alchemy.

This is not all. According to Zhao Yizhen, the "external" and the "internal" domains in turn have an "internal" and an "external" aspect.[73] Controlling one's emotional nature (*qing*) so that it focuses on one's original nature (*xing*) pertains to the order of the "external"; allowing this original nature return to the Origin pertains to the "internal" domain. One could say that the external pertains to the behavior and the internal to the mystical ascesis, and that here again we are facing two stages or sides of the Work. But the master adds that when the original nature is quiet and the emotional nature is empty, "then one neither moves nor is motionless; there is no more internal or external", and this is called "internal and external in the Internal Elixir." This concerns the plane of the Internal Elixir, which is the mental and psychological level of the human being. It is complemented by the External Elixir, where the alchemical metaphors are used. In this External Elixir, one must "internally" maintain the "liquor of Wood," and "externally" use the true Lead to master it. When the Internal and the External Medicines are mastered, one abandons the External Medicine, and there is no more internal or

[73] *Yuanyang zi fayu*, 1.1a-2a.

external, "This is what we call internal and external in the External Elixir." The author adds: "The inner light is subtle and wondrous, formless and nameless. The saintly masters could only lend it names [borrowed] from the External Elixir."

Li Daochun's discourse seems to contradict what we have just seen. Yet Chen Zhixu relies on him for a part of his speech on the *neidan* and the *waidan*, without any apparent difficulty. According to Li Daochun, in fact, the External Medicine is the essence, the breath, and the gross human intellect; the Internal Medicine is the particle of original Yang.[74] However, Li Daochun agrees with other texts when he deems the External Medicine to concern the work on the *ming* (vital force) and the physiological techniques that grant only longevity. The Internal Medicine comes next, with the work on the *xing*, which is the maturation of True Yang "without action." On the one hand, says Li Daochun, there is the External Medicine formed out of Yin and Yang, which come and go and on which one should work by means of breathing and mental techniques. On the other hand, there is the Internal Medicine, which is Kan and Li placed at the center.[75] This is identical to what we have seen above. It seems to me that here Li Daochun is looking at things from a practical standpoint: the External Medicine is the result of the work done on the human coarse elements, which need to be refined in order to extract the cosmic and primordial elements.

That this is only a difference in wording due to a different standpoint is confirmed by another passage in Li Daochun's text. There he takes a broader point of view that surpasses the distinction between "external" and "internal," and arranges the alchemical Work into three stages (*guan*, lit., "barriers"). Li Daochun states that the first stage consists in collecting the original Yan; the second one in "repairing" the Yin; and the third one in reaching Emptiness.[76]

Li Daochun's charts are of remarkable interest.[77] The chart of the External Medicine (see fig. 1) is reversed compared to the chart of the Fire regime (see fig. 2). Their structure is the same, but they mirror one another (we return here to the theme of reflection). The inversion is horizontal: for the External Medicine, the upward movement is

[74] *Zhonghe ji*, 2.4a-6b, and 3.25a and 28a.
[75] *Id.*, 3.32a.
[76] *Id.*, 2.6b-7a.
[77] *Id.*, 2.2a-3b.

made toward the right, and the downward movement is made toward the left; vice versa for the Fire regime. The sites of the course of breath are inverted in a similar way. The Fire regime, associated by some authors with the internal phase of the Work, here seems to be an intermediate phase, and the Internal Medicine appears to be its completion.

The chart of the Internal Medicine (see fig. 3) differs in two main respects from the chart of the External Medicine. The lower part (representing the foundation of the Work) is marked as *wuwei* (non-action), instead of *youwei* (action) that is inscribed at the bottom of the chart of the External Medicine. In addition, the center is Kun (pure Yin) for the External Medicine, and Qian (pure Yang) for the Internal Medicine. But this central Qian is enclosed above and below by the trigrams Li and Kan, and then by Qian and Kun, in accordance with the dual, encased arrangements prior and posterior to Heaven.

According to the same text,[78] this corresponds to the Internal Medicine that, being the final stage, overlaps the last stage of the External Medicine. Both stages consist in "purifying the spirit" (*lian-shen*), in making "body and spirit equally wondrous" (a stock phrase of the alchemists), and in returning to the Dao. This paragraph of Li Daochun's work is followed by another paragraph devoted to the Great Medicine, which in its "operating" (*yong*) aspect includes an "internal" and an "external," but in its deeper substance (*ti*) consists of "the great affair of the three original principles (*sanyuan*)."

As we have seen, according to the point of view that we adopt and that gives meaning to the words, the formulations may conflict with one another. One can say, for example, that the *waidan* is obtained in one instant if this refers to the flash of awakening that allows one to capture the "external" Yang, the instant of consciousness that arises in the complete silence of thoughts, and that is equivalent to the state prior to Heaven, when the *Taiji* is not yet divided. The *neidan*, on the contrary, is the time of maturation and development of this Yang; it is the Fire regime and therefore requires ten symbolic months of gestation. But this does not prevent the *waidan* made of an instant of light from being achieved by means of long practices of circulation of the breath and meditation. Therefore, some alchemists, such as Li Daochun and Chen Zhixu, consider the first stage to be action and

[78] *Id.*, 2.5a.

the second one to be non-action. Others, like Yu Yan, maintain that the first step is non-action, because one should be innerly empty and thus summon the cosmic Breath.[79]

As Xia Zongyu explains, in terms of the *waidan* every step imposed by the Fire regime is required; but in terms of the *neidan*, no such distinction can exist, because time applies only to the *waidan*. The point of view of non-action operates here: things occur by themselves.[80]

CONCLUSION

As we have seen, the term External Elixir originally designates the metaphoric language of "internal alchemy." *Waidan* has denoted not only laboratory alchemy in contrast to inner ascesis or to physiological exercises, but also the new discipline that we call internal alchemy, in contrast to the earlier physiological or meditation techniques. Now, one of the main and most apparent features of this new discipline is the use of the language of operative alchemy. It is therefore the language proper to this discipline that is referred to as *waidan*, as it makes it possible to speak of the ascesis and the mystical discipline, and thus to manifest and transmit the mystical experience. This ascesis, however, involves two sides, or steps, closely related to one another: one is physiological, and consists of the work on the *ming* and the *qing*, the vital and passional forces of the human being, which it must manage. This is the external facet. The other side is deeper, mental, and "spiritual"; it is the internal facet, and consists of the work on the *xing*. These distinctions, nevertheless, are extinguished in the Great Vehicle and the Great Medicine.

A good illustration and a good summary of the relation between *nei* and *wai* can be found in a formulation of the *Jindan zhizhi* (Straightforward Directions on the Golden Elixir): "The *xing* (true nature) comes from the *ming* (vital force), and the *ming* returns to the *xing*."[81] The *xing* is defined as being drawn from the *ming*; it is the *waiyao*, the External Medicine taken from Kan ☵. The *xing* returning to the *ming* is the *neiyao*, the Internal Medicine. The internalization

[79] *Zhouyi cantong qi fahui*, 5.3b and 8a.
[80] *Ziyang zhenren wuzhen pian jiangyi*, 4.5a.
[81] *Jindan zhizhi* (preface dated 1250), 3b.

of the External Medicine becomes the Internal Medicine; the *ming* is extracted from the *xing* and returns to the *xing*. As the alchemists say, the child extracted from its mother in turn contains its mother in its womb.

This is simply one aspect of the fundamental reversal that occurs in alchemy. It is a reversal of encasings: the content, the *xing*, becomes the container; at the same time, and again paradoxically, this "content" was external but becomes internal by becoming the container. The Dragon and the Tiger contain one another.[82] There is an external Yang, which is the True Yang prior to Heaven. Being pure, it is Qian ☰. But it can apprehended in our "posterior" world only as contained within the Yin, as the inner line of Kan ☵. Therefore the external Yang is also our internal Yang contained within the Yin. Similarly, an equation is made among the Great Yin and the emerging Yang that it generates, the "great quiescence" of concentration, and the "light that appears in the room," a term that the alchemists borrow from the *Zhuangzi*, which connotes the emerging Yang, the beginning of the movement of the Work.[83]

Therefore we can have the equation Great Yin = inner line of Kan = emerging Yang, as well as the equation Great Yang = inner Yang within Kan. This justifies and explains the term "Qian-Metal" (*qian-jin*) used by the alchemists, an expression that conjoins the pure Yang-Qian and the Metal that stands for Kan, i.e., the Yang within the Yin. According to Li Daochun, this "Qian-Metal" is simply the "Water-Metal" (*shuijin*, another name of Mercury), pure Yin-Water and Metal. This implies an equation between Great Yin and Metal (at the same time its son and its mother), on the one hand, and between this couple and the one formed by pure Yang and Metal-Kan, Yang within Yin, on the other.[84]

In their way of expressing themselves, the alchemists deliberately employ a continuous overlap between the "static" state of the pure concepts (Qian and Kun, internal and external, pure Yin and Yang, etc.) and their dynamic state, the transformations of the ones into the others, the interchanges that necessarily take place and are the pur-

---

[82] See, for example, *Zhouyi cantong qi fenzhang tong zhenyi*, 2.22a.

[83] [*Zhuangzi*, chapter 4; trans. Watson, *The Complete Works of Chuang Tzu*, p. 58: "Look into that closed room, the empty chamber where brightness is born!"— Ed.]

[84] *Id.*, 2.5a.

pose of their Work. The disjunction that occurs to create the cosmos and the world of language is immediately followed by a reconjunction; and the alchemical Work consists in making all those images play dynamically, in causing the rise and the descent of the Yin and the Yang, of the Yin within the Yang and the Yang within the Yin, and in extracting one from the other.

Therefore we cannot really define any term; its definition vanishes into its dynamic function, and its function is to change. We can only show how a term functions.

MEANINGS ASSIGNED TO THE TERMS
NEI (INTERNAL) AND *WAI* (EXTERNAL)

References are to the number of sections and subsections in this essay.

Wai (External)	*Nei* (Internal)
I.1 Coarse breath of food	True Breath
I.2 Cosmic primordial Breath	Personal primordial Breath
I.3 Astral meditations	Physiological practices
I.4 Yang Elixir	Yin Elixir
Ascension to Heaven	Longevity
Circulation of Breath	Guarding the One, etc.
I.5a Symbols: Dragon, Tiger	Breathing exercises
I.5b Essences of Wood and Metal	Heart, kidneys
Yin-Yang, trigrams, five agents	Various longevity techniques
Lead, Mercury	
Immortality	Happiness and peace
I.5c Tiger, Dragon	Circulation of breath
Essences of Wood and Metal	Bodily spirits
I.6. Symbolic alchemical language	Human body
Cosmic primordial Breath	Circulation of breath-humors

II.1   Breath of True Yang

Essence of Wood and Metal, Red Lead,
Black Mercury

II.2   Yang within Yin

Yin within Yang

Inner line of Kan ☵

Inner line of Li ☲

II.3   First stage: Extraction

Second stage: Fire regime

Yang Elixir

Yin Elixir

Extraction of prior Yang

Reparation of Yin by this Yang

Action, *you* (existence)

Non-action, *wu* (emptiness)

(or vice versa in certain instances)

Ming (vital force)

Xing (innate inner nature)

Earthly

Celestial

"The other"

"Me"

South-West, Moon, Kun ☷

North-West, body, Qian ☰

"Host"

"Guest"

Essence of Metal, Lead

Essence of Wood, Mercury

Tables and Pictures

Table 1

	WOOD	FIRE	SOIL	METAL	WATER
DIRECTIONS	east	south	center	west	north
SEASONS	spring	summer	(midsummer)	autumn	winter
COLORS	green	red	yellow	white	black
EMBLEMATIC ANIMALS	green dragon	vermilion sparrow	yellow dragon	white tiger	snake and turtle
NUMBERS	3, 8	2, 7	5, 10	4, 9	1, 6
YIN-YANG (1)	minor Yang	great Yang	balance	minor Yin	great Yin
YIN-YANG (2)	True Yin	Yang	balance	True Yang	Yin
STEMS	*jia* 甲 *yi* 乙	*bing* 丙 *ding* 丁	*wu* 戊 *ji* 己	*geng* 庚 *xin* 辛	*ren* 壬 *gui* 癸
BRANCHES	*yin* 寅 *mao* 卯	*wu* 午 *si* 巳	*xu* 戌, *chou* 丑 *wei* 未, *chen* 辰	*you* 酉 *shen* 申	*hai* 亥 *zi* 子
PLANETS	Jupiter	Mars	Saturn	Venus	Mercury
RELATIONS	father	daughter	ancestors	mother	son
VISCERA	liver	heart	spleen	lungs	kidneys
BODY ORGAN	eyes	tongue	mouth	nose	ears

The five agents (*wuxing*) and their associations.

Table 2

FIRE
South
Vermilion Sparrow
2
cinnabar
Original Spirit (*yuanshen* 元神)

WOOD	SOIL	METAL
East	Center	West
Green Dragon		White Tiger
3	5	4
True Mercury		True Lead
inner nature (*xing* 性)	intention (*yi* 意)	qualities (*qing* 情)

WATER
North
Dark Warrior
1
black lead
Original Essence (*yuanjing* 元精)

Spatial arrangement of the five agents (*wuxing* 五行),
with some of their main associations.
In agreement with traditional Chinese conventions,
this and the following tables show the North at the bottom,
the South at the top, the East on the left, and the West on the right.

Table 3

	GENERATES	IS GENERATED BY	CONQUERS	IS CONQUERED BY
WATER	Wood	Metal	Fire	Soil
WOOD	Fire	Water	Soil	Metal
FIRE	Soil	Wood	Metal	Water
SOIL	Metal	Fire	Water	Wood
METAL	Water	Soil	Wood	Fire

"Generation" (*xiangsheng* 相生)
and "conquest" (*xiangke* 相剋)
sequences of the five agents (*wuxing* 五行).

Table 4

AGENT	GENERATIVE NUMBER	ACHIEVED NUMBER
WATER	1	6
FIRE	2	7
WOOD	3	8
METAL	4	9
SOIL	5	10

"Generative numbers" (*shengshu* 生數)
and "achieved numbers" (*chengshu* 成數)
of the five agents.

Table 5

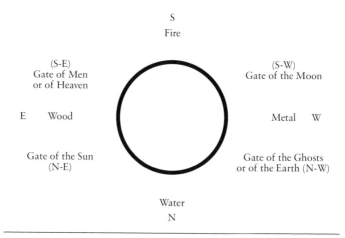

Spatial arrangement of the four external agents
and the four gates. In agreement with traditional Chinese conventions,
this and the following tables show the North at the bottom,
the South at the top, the East on the left, and the West on the right.

Table 6

☰	☱	☲	☳	☴	☵	☶	☷
乾	兌	離	震	巽	坎	艮	坤
QIAN	DUI	LI	ZHEN	XUN	KAN	GEN	KUN
heaven	lake	fire	thunder	wind	water	mountain	earth
father	youngest daughter	second daughter	eldest son	eldest daughter	second son	youngest son	mother
south	southeast	east	northeast	southwest	west	northwest	north
northwest	west	south	east	southeast	north	northeast	southwest

The eight trigrams (*bagua* 八卦) and their main
associations. From top to bottom: elements in nature, family relations, and
directions in the cosmological
configurations "prior to Heaven" (*xiantian* 先天)
and "posterior to Heaven" (*houtian* 後天).

Table 7

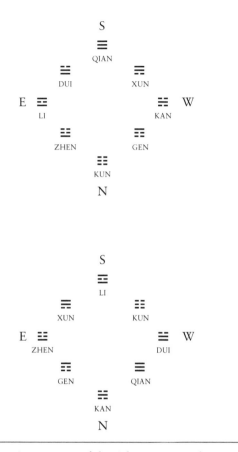

Arrangement of the eight trigrams in the
configurations "prior to Heaven" (*xiantian*, top) and "posterior to
Heaven" (*houtian*, bottom).

Table 8

	STEMS		AGENTS	DIRECTIONS	COLORS	VISCERA	NUMBERS
1	jia	甲					
			WOOD	east	green	liver	3, 8
2	yi	乙					
3	bing	丙					
			FIRE	south	red	heart	2, 7
4	ding	丁					
5	wu	戊					
			SOIL	center	yellow	spleen	5
6	ji	己					
7	geng	庚					
			METAL	west	white	lungs	4, 9
8	xin	辛					
9	ren	壬					
			WATER	north	black	kidneys	1, 6
10	gui	癸					

The ten celestial stems (*tiangan*) and their associations.

Table 9

	BRANCHES		AGENTS	DIRECTIONS	HOURS	NUMBERS
1	zi	子	WATER	N	23–1	1, 6
2	chou	丑	SOIL	NNE 3/4 E	1–3	5, 10
3	yin	寅	WOOD	ENE 3/4 N	3–5	3, 8
4	mao	卯	WOOD	E	5–7	3, 8
5	chen	辰	SOIL	ESE 3/4 S	7–9	5, 10
6	si	巳	FIRE	SSE 3/4 E	9–11	2, 7
7	wu	午	FIRE	S	11–13	2, 7
8	wei	未	SOIL	SSW 3/4 W	13–15	5, 10
9	shen	申	METAL	WSW 3/4 S	15–17	4, 9
10	you	酉	METAL	W	17–19	4, 9
11	xu	戌	SOIL	WNW 3/4 N	19–21	5, 10
12	hai	亥	WATER	NNW 3/4 W	21–23	1, 6

The twelve earthly branches (*dizhi*) and their associations.

Figures 1-3

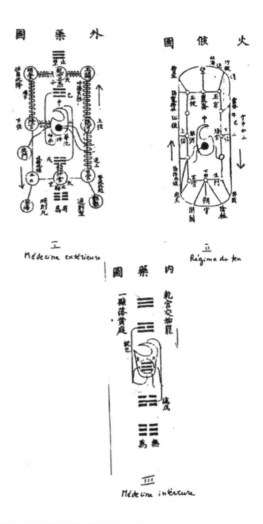

Top left: "Chart of the External Medicine" ("Waiyao tu").
Top right: "Chart of the Fire Regime" ("Huohou tu").
Bottom: "Chart of the Internal Medicine" ("Neiyao tu").
Li Daochun, *Zhonghe ji*, chapter 2.

Appendix

Works by Isabelle Robinet

1976   "Randonnées extatiques des taoïstes dans les astres." *Monumenta Serica* 32: 159–273.

1977   *Les commentaires du Tao tö king jusqu'au VIIe siècle*. Paris: Collège de France, Institut des Hautes Études Chinoises.

1979   *Méditation taoïste*. Paris: Dervy Livres, 1979. [Translated into English as *Taoist Meditation: The Mao-shan Tradition of Great Purity* (Albany: State University of New York Press, 1993).]

1979   "Introduction au *Kieou-tchen tchong-king*." *Society for the Study of Chinese Religions Bulletin* 7: 24–45.

1979   "Metamorphosis and Deliverance from the Corpse in Taoism." *History of Religions* 19: 37–70.

1983   "Kouo Siang ou le monde comme absolu." *T'oung Pao* 69: 87–112.

1983   "Le *Ta-tung chen-ching*; son authenticité et sa place dans les textes du Shang-ch'ing ching." In Michael Strickmann, ed. *Tantric and Taoist Studies in Honour of Rolf A. Stein*, II:394–433. Bruxelles: Institut Belge des Hautes Études Chinoises.

1983   "Chuang-tzu et le taoïsme 'religieux.'" *Journal of Chinese Religions* 11: 59–109.

1984   Entries in Denis Huisman, ed., *Dictionnaire des philosophes*. Paris: Presses Universitaires de France.

1984   *La révélation du Shangqing dans l'histoire du taoïsme*. 2 vols. Paris: École Française d'Extrême-Orient.

1984   "Notes préliminaires sur quelques antinomies fondamentales entre le bouddhisme et le taoïsme." In Lionello Lanciotti, ed., *Incontro di religioni in Asia tra il III e il X secolo d.C*, 217–42. Firenze: Leo S. Olschki Editore.

1985   "*Jing, qi* et *shen*." *Revue française d'acupuncture* 43: 27–36.

1985   "L'unité transcendante des trois enseignements selon les taoïstes des Sung et des Yüan." In Gert Naundorf, Karl-Heinz Pohl, and Hans-Herman Schmidt, eds., *Religion und Philosophie in Ostasien:*

Appendix

	Festschrift für Hans Steininger zum 65. Geburtstag, 103–26. Würzburg: Königshausen und Neumann.
1985	"Polysémisme du texte canonique et syncrétisme des interprétations: Étude taxonomique des commentaires du *Daode jing* au sein de la tradition chinoise." *Extrême-Orient — Extrême-Occident* 5: 27–47. Revised English version: "Later Commentaries: Textual Polysemy and Syncretistic Interpretations," in Livia Kohn and Michael LaFargue, eds., *Lao-tzu and the Tao-te-ching*, 119–42 (Albany: State University of New York Press, 1998).
1986	"L'alchimie interne dans le taoïsme." *Cahiers d'Extrême-Asie* 2: 241–52.
1986	"La notion du *hsing* dans le taoïsme et son rapport avec celle du confucianisme." *Journal of the American Oriental Society* 106: 183–96.
1986	"The Taoist Immortal: Jesters of Light and Shadow, Heaven and Earth." *Journal of Chinese Religions* 13–14: 87–105.
1986	"La pratique du Tao, la transmission des textes sacrés, les paradis terrestres et cosmiques, la marche sur les étoiles." In A. Akoun, ed., *Mythes et croyances du monde entier*, 369–98. Paris: Lidis.
1988	"Sexualité et taoïsme." In Marcel Bernos, ed., *Sexualité et religion*, 51–71. Paris: Les Éditions du Cerf.
1989	"L'unité complexe de la pensée chinoise." In André Jacob, ed., *Encyclopédie philosophique universelle*, vol. 1: *L'Univers philosophique*, 1595–99. Paris: Presses Universitaires de France.
1989	"Taoïsme et mystique." *Cahiers d'études chinoises* 8: 65–103.
1989	"Original Contributions of *Neidan* to Taoism and Chinese Thought." In Livia Kohn, ed., *Taoist Meditation and Longevity Techniques*, 297–330. Ann Arbor: Center for Chinese Studies, University of Michigan.
1989	"Visualization and Ecstatic Flight in Shangqing Taoism." In Livia Kohn, ed., *Taoist Meditation and Longevity Techniques*, 159–91. Ann Arbor: Center for Chinese Studies, University of Michigan.
1989–90	"Recherche sur l'alchimie intérieure (*neidan*): L'école Zhenyuan." *Cahiers d'Extrême-Asie* 5: 141–62.
1990	"Nature et rôle du maître spirituel dans le taoïsme non liturgique." In Michel Meslin, ed., *Maîtres et disciples dans les traditions religieuses*, 37–51. Paris: Les Éditions du Cerf.
1990	"The Place and Meaning of the Notion of *Taiji* in Taoist Sources Prior to the Ming Dynasty." *History of Religions* 29: 373–411.
1991	*Histoire du Taoïsme des origines au XIVe siècle*. Paris: Les Éditions du Cerf. [Translated into English as *Taoism: Growth of a Religion* (Stanford: Stanford University Press, 1997).]

114

1991	"Sur le sens des termes *waidan* et *neidan*." *Taoist Resources* 3.1: 3–40.
1992	"Il demiurgo taoista." *Quaderni di agopuntura tradizionale* 12.1–2: 1–12; 13.1–2: 1–10.
1992	"Des Changements et de l'Invariable." In Charles Le Blanc et Rémi Mathieu, eds., *Mythe et philosophie a l'aube de la Chine impériale: Études sur le Huainan zi*, 3–15. Montréal: Presses de l'Université de Montréal.
1992	"Le monde à l'envers dans l'alchimie intérieure taoïste." *Revue de l'Histoire des Religions* 209: 239–57.
1992	135 entries in André Jacob, ed., *Encyclopédie philosophique universelle*, vol. 3: *Les oeuvres philosophiques: dictionnaire*. Paris: Presses Universitaires de France.
1993	"Le monde merveilleux du taoïsme mystique et le thème du retour à l'Origine." *Cahiers de L'Herne*, 1993: 287–301.
1993	"Mystique et rationalité: Le langage dans l'alchimie intérieure taoïste ou l'effort pour dire le contradictoire." *Asiatische Studien / Études asiatiques* 47: 645–62.
1993	*Les grands traités du Huainan zi*, with Claude Larre and Elisabeth Rochat de la Vallée. Paris: Institut Ricci, Les Éditions du Cerf.
1994	"Le rôle et le sens des nombres dans la cosmologie et l'alchimie taoïstes." *Extrême-Orient — Extrême-Occident* 16: 93–120.
1994	"Primus movens et création récurrente." *Taoist Resources* 5.2: 29–70.
1995	"Un, deux, trois: Les différentes modalités de l'Un et sa dynamique." *Cahiers d'Extrême-Asie* 8: 175–220.
1995	*Introduction à l'alchimie intérieure taoïste: De l'unité et de la multiplicité. Avec une traduction commentée des Versets de l'éveil à la Vérité*. Paris: Les Éditions du Cerf.
1995	"Les marches cosmiques et les carrés magiques dans le taoïsme." *Journal of Chinese Religions* 23: 81–94.
1996	"*Neidan*" [Internal alchemy]. *Zhongguo wenshi yanjiu tongji* 6.1: 11–29.
1996	"Une lecture du *Zhuangzi*." *Études chinoises* 15: 109–58.
1996	*Lao zi et le Tao*. Paris: Bayard Éditions.
1997	Five articles in Frédéric Lenoir and Ysé Tardan-Masquelier, eds., *Encyclopédie des religions*. Paris: Bayard. ["Zhuang zi," 1054; "Chine: L'équilibre du yin et du yang," 1661–65; "Chine: L'homme cosmique," 1707–11; "Chine: Le mal dans la pensée chinoise," 1736–41; "Chine: Le salut chinoise ou l'insertion du microcosme dans le macrocosme," 1770–76; "Chine: Les vertus confucéennes," 1811–16.]

1997 "Genèses: Au début, il n'y a pas d'avant." In Jacques Gernet and Marc Kalinowski, eds., *En suivant la Voie Royale: Mélanges en hommage à Léon Vandermeersch*, 121–40. Paris: École Française d'Extrême-Orient.

1998 "La 'Mère' et la 'Femelle obscure' de Laozi." In Michel Cazenave, ed., *La face féminine de Dieu*, 137–67. Paris: Noésis.

1998 Seven entries in Jean Servier, ed., *Dictionnaire critique de l'ésotérisme*. Paris: Presses Universitaires de France. ["Les textes sacrés"; "La construction de l'autel"; "La contemplation intérieure"; "Les randonnées extatiques"; "État antérieur au Ciel et état postérieure au Ciel"; "Alchimie intérieure" (with Monica Esposito); "Sans limite et Limite suprême, Wuji et Taiji"]

1998 "Later Commentaries: Textual Polysemy and Syncretistic Interpretations." In Livia Kohn and Michael LaFargue, eds, *Lao-tzu and the Tao-te-ching*, 119–42. Albany: State University of New York Press.

1999 "Les voies du comparativisme: La Chine et la philosophie gréco-occidentale" and "La cosmologie chinoise." In André Jacob, ed., *Encyclopédie philosophique universelle*, vol. 4: *Le discours philosophique*. Paris: Presses Universitaires de France.

1999 "The diverse interpretations of the *Laozi*." In Mark Csikszentmiha-lyi and Philip J. Ivanhoe, eds., *Religious and Philosophical Aspects of the Laozi*, 127–61. Albany: State University of New York Press.

1999 Three chapters in Flora Blanchon, Isabelle Robinet, Jacques Giès, and André Kneib, *Arts et histoire de la Chine*, vol. 2. Paris: Presses de l'Université de Paris-Sorbonne. ["Le taoïsme pendant la dynastie Han"; "L'École du Mystère et les courants taoïstes"; "Le Boud-dhisme."]

1999 "Lun *Taiyi sheng shui*" [On the *Taiyi sheng shui*]. Translated by Edmund Ryden. *Daojia wenhua yanjiu*, 17: 332–39.

2000 "Shangqing: Highest Clarity." In Livia Kohn, ed., *Daoism Handbook*, 196–224. Leiden: E. J. Brill.

2002 "Genesis and Pre-cosmic Eras in Daoism." In Lee Cheuk Yin and Chan Man Sing eds., *Daoyuan binfen lu (A Daoist Florilegium: A Festschrift Dedicated to Professor Liu Ts'un-yan)*, 144–84. Hong Kong: Shangwu yinshuguan, 2002.

2004 "L'eau et le feu dans le taoïsme." In G. Capdeville, ed., *L'eau et le feu dans les religions antiques*. Paris: De Boccard.

2004 192 entries in Kristofer Schipper and Franciscus Verellen, eds., *The Taoist Canon: A Historical Companion to the Daozang*. Chicago: Chicago University Press.

2007 59 entries in Fabrizio Pregadio, ed., *The Encyclopedia of Taoism*. London: Routledge.

Glossary of Chinese Characters

Bai Yuchan 白玉蟾

bajie 八節 ("eight joints")

bao 包 ("to contain")

bei 備 ("complete")

ben 本 ("fundamentally")

benzhu 本注 ("original commentary")

bi 彼 ("that," "the other")

Cantong qi 參同契 (Token for Joining the Three)

chan 產 ("emergence")

chen 辰 ("marks")

Chen Nan 陳楠

Chen Pu 陳朴

Chen xiansheng neidan jue 陳先生內丹訣 (Instructions on the Internal Elixir by Master Chen)

Chen Zhixu 陳致虛

cheng 成 ("achieved" numbers)

ci 此 ("this")

cuancu 攢簇 ("concentration")

Cuixu pian 翠虛篇 (The Emerald Emptiness)

cun 存 ("to give presence")

dadan 大丹 (Great Elixir)

dafu 大夫 (high official)

Dai Qizong 戴起宗

Daode jing 道德經 (Book of the Way and its Virtue)

Daofa huiyuan 道法會元 (Collected Essentials of Taoist Methods)

Daozang jiyao 道藏輯要

dayao 大藥 (Great Medicine)

dian 點 ("to project")

diandao 顛倒 ("reversal, inversion")

dongtian 洞天 (Grotto-Heavens)

dou 斗 ("bushel")

dunjia 遁甲 (Hidden Stem)

Duren jing 度人經 (Scripture on Salvation)

fa 法 (Dharma)

fangshi 方士 ("men possessing recipes")

fashen 法身 ("body of the law," *dharmakāya*)

fu 府 ("receptacles")

fudi 福地 (Blissful Lands)

geng 庚 (one of the ten celestial stems)

gongfu 功夫 ("work")

guan 官 ("officers")

guan 關 ("barrier," a stage of the alchemical practice)

Guanshiyin 觀世音

Guanyin 觀音

gui Yang 癸陽

Han Po 韓博

Hanshu 漢書 (History of the Former Han Dynasty)

hao 號 ("to be named")

Hongfan 洪範 (The Great Plan)

hou 候 (a unit of time)

houtian 後天 ("posterior to heaven" or "to the world")

hu xi huang xi 忽兮恍兮 ("vague and indistinct")

Huainan zi 淮南子 (Book of the Master of Huainan)

huandan 還丹 (Cyclical Elixir)

Huang Ziru 黃自如

huanghu 恍忽 ("vague and indistinct")

117

Huanzhen ji 還真集 (Anthology of Reverting to Reality)
huawei 化為 ("to transform into")
hui 慧 (wisdom)
Huisi 慧思
hun 魂 ("Yang soul")
Hunyuan bajing zhenjing 混元八景真經 (True Scripture of the Eight Luminous Spirits of the Inchoate Origin)
huohou 火候 (Fire regime)
"Huohou tu" 火候圖 ("Chart of the Fire Regime")
huoshu 火數 ("numbers of fire")
ji 即 (grammatical marker of copula)
jia 假 ("to borrow")
jiaming 假名 ("to borrow the name of")
jie 節 (a unit of time)
jin 斤 ("pound," a unit of weight)
Jin yuechi 金鑰匙 (Golden Key)
Jindan 金丹 (Golden Elixir)
Jindan dayao 金丹大要 (Great Essentials of the Golden Elixir)
Jindan sibai zi 金丹四百字 (Four Hundred Words on the Golden Elixir)
Jindan zhizhi 金丹直指 (Straightforward Directions on the Golden Elixir)
jing 景 (luminous celestial spirits)
jing 精 (essence)
Jing Fang 京方
jinjing 金精 (Essence of Metal)
jinye huandan 金液還丹 (Golden Liquor and Cyclical Elixir)
jiu 九 ("nine")
jiu 究 ("exhaustion")
ju 聚 ("to gather" or "to collect")
kan-wu 坎戊
ke 克 ("to conquest")
ke 刻 (a unit of time)
ke 客 ("guest")
koan 公案 (*gong'an*)

kun xiantian qi 坤先天氣 (Breath prior to Heaven of Kun)
Laozi 老子
li 理 ("principles")
li 里 ("mile")
Li Daochun 李道純
li-ji 離己
liang 兩 ("ounce," a unit of weight)
liangyi 兩儀 ("two principles")
lianshen 鍊神 ("purifying the spirit")
liao 了 ("transcendence")
Liezi 列子 (Book of Master Lie)
ling gan 靈感 ("divine animation")
Lingbao 靈寶 (Numinous Treasure)
Lingbao jun 靈寶君
liuding 六丁 (Six Ding)
liuhe 六合 ("six conjunctions")
liuji 六極 ("six poles")
liujia 六甲 (Six Jia)
liumo 六漠 ("six deserts")
liuwei 六位 (six hexagrams lines)
Lu Ziye 陸子野
lü 呂 (pitch pipes)
Lü Dongbin 呂洞賓
luo 絡 (vessels)
man 滿 ("full")
manzu 滿足 ("complete, sufficient")
mao 卯 (one of the twelve earthly branches)
Meng Xi 孟喜
ming 名 ("to be named")
ming 命 ("vital force")
ming 明 ("comprehension")
Mingtang 明堂 (Hall of Light)
mo 脈 (arteries)
Mu Changzhao 牧常晁
muye 木液 (Liquor of Wood)
nayin 納因 ("induced sounds")
nei 內 ("internal")
Neidan, *neidan* 內丹 (internal alchemy, "internal elixir")
neishi 內事 ("inner practice")
neiyao 內藥 (Internal Medicine)
"Neiyao tu" 內藥圖 "Chart of the

Internal Medicine")

ni 逆 ("going backward," "going against the current")

ning shen ru yu kan qi 凝神入於坤臍

Niwan xiansheng 泥丸先生

Peng Xiao 彭曉

po 魄 ("Yin soul")

qi 器 ("instrument"; "material entity")

qi 氣 (1. breath; 2. a unit of time)

qian houtian qi 乾後天氣

Qian zuodu 乾鑿度 (Opening the Way to the Understanding of Qian ䷀)

qianjin 乾金 ("Qian-Metal")

qing 情 ("emotional nature")

Qiu Chuji 邱處機

quan 全 ("making full")

ren 仁 ("humanity")

Sandong zhunang 三洞珠囊 (Pearl Satchel of the Three Caverns)

Sanhuang 三皇

sanjiao 三焦 ("three burners")

Sanyuan, *sanyuan* 三元 (Three Primes; three major deities of the body)

seshen 色身 ("appearance body," *rūpakāya*)

sexiang 色相 ("forms")

Shangdong xindan jingjue 上洞心丹經訣 (Instructions on the Scripture of the Heart Elixir of the Highest Cavern)

Shangqing 上清

Shangyang zi 上陽子

Shao Yong 邵雍

shen 神 (spirit)

Shenbao jun 神寶君

sheng 生 (1. "to generate"; 2. "emergent" or "generative" numbers)

shenqi 神氣 ("divine breaths")

shi 是 (grammatical marker of copula)

shi . . . ye 是 . . . 也 (copula, grammatical pattern for a definition, e.g., "X is Y")

shishi 識時 ("qualities and times")

shiyin 世音

shuijin 水金 (Metal of the Water; "Water-Metal," i.e., mercury)

shuiyin 水銀 (mercury)

shun 順 (going in the "right" sense)

Shuogua 説卦 (Explanation of the Trigrams)

sitai 四太 ("four greats")

Taichu 太初 (Great Beginning)

Taiji 太極 (Great Ultimate)

Taiping jing 太平經 (Scripture of Great Peace)

Taishang jiuyao xinyin miaojing 太上九要心印妙經 (Most High Wondrous Scripture of the Mind Seal and Its Nine Essentials)

Taishi 太始 (Great Commencement)

Taisu 太素 (Great Purity)

Taiyi 太易 (Great Simplicity)

Taiyin 太陰 (Great Yin)

Tao Zhi 陶植

ti 體 ("substance," "constitutive basis," "body")

tian 天 (Heaven, Nature)

Tianbao jun 天寶君

tishu 體數 ("fundamental number")

wai 外 ("external")

Waidan, *waidan* 外丹 (external alchemy, "external elixir")

Waidan neidan lun 外丹內丹論 (Treatise on the External and the Internal Elixirs)

Waiguo fangpin 外國放品 (Distribution of the Outer Realms)

waiwu 外物 ("external things")

waixiang 外象 ("external symbols")

waiyao 外藥 (External Medicine)

"Waiyao tu" 外藥圖 ("Chart of the External Medicine")

Wang Bi 王弼

Wang Dao 王道

wei 為 (grammatical marker of copula)

wei 衛 ("defense")

wei 謂 ("to be named")
Weng Baoguang 翁葆光
wo 我 ("me")
wu 午 (one of the twelve earthly branches)
wu 無 ("non-being," "non-existence")
wu 物 ("thing")
Wu Chongxu 伍冲虛
Wu Wu 吳悟
wuwei 無為 ("non-action")
wuxiang 無象 ("having no image")
wuxing 五行 (five agents)
"Wuxing tu" 五行圖 ("Chart of the Five Agents")
Wuzhen pian 悟真篇 (Awakening to Reality)
Xia Zongyu 夏宗宇
xiang 象 ("image," "symbol," "metaphor")
xiangke 相剋 ("conquest" sequence of the five agents)
xiangsheng 相生 ("generation" sequence of the five agents)
xiangshu 象數 ("images and numbers")
xiangying 相應 ("to respond to one another")
Xianquan ji 峴泉集 (Anthology of Mountain Springs)
xiantian 先天 ("prior to heaven" or "to the world")
Xiantian xuanmiao yunü taishang shengmu zichuan xiandao 先天玄妙玉女太上聖母資傳仙道 (The Way of Immortality Transmitted by the Most High Holy Mother, Precelestial Jade Woman of Obscure Mystery)
Xiao Yanzhi 蕭延芝
Xici 繫辭 ("Great Appendix" to the *Book of Changes*)
xin 心 (heart, the intuitive spirit)
xing 性 ("true nature," "original nature")

xing 行 ("practice")
xing dao 行道 ("implementation of the Dao")
Xiudan miaoyong zhili lun 修丹妙用至理論 (Treatise on the Ultimate Principles of the Wondrous Operation of the Cultivation of the Elixir)
xiuding 修定 (concentration)
Xiuzhen bijue 修真祕訣 (Secret Instructions on the Cultivation of Reality)
xuanji 玄極 ("hidden spring")
Xuanxue 玄學 ("school of the Mystery")
Xuanzong zhizhi wanfa tonggui 玄宗直指萬法同歸 (Reintegrating the Ten Thousand Dharmas: A Straightforward Explanation of the Taoist Tradition)
xubi 虛比 ("empty similitudes")
Xue Daoguang 薛道光
yangdan 陽丹 (Yang Elixir)
yangsheng 養生 ("nourishing life")
Yanluo zi 煙蘿子
ye 也 (grammatical marker of copula)
Ye Shibiao 葉士表
Ye Wenshu 葉文叔
yi 意 ("creative idea")
yi 義 ("righteousness")
Yijing 易經 (Book of Changes)
Yimen pomi ge 夷門破迷歌 (Yimen's Song on Overcoming Delusion)
Yin Xi 尹喜
yindan 陰丹 (Yin Elixir)
ying 營 ("construction")
yinyang wuxing 陰陽五行 (Yin-Yang and five agents)
yishen 移神 ("carrying one's spirit")
yong 用 ("operation," "implementation," "functioning")
you 有 ("being," "existence")
you 酉 (one of the twelve earthly branches)

youming 窈冥 ("dark and obscure")

youwei 有為 ("action")

yu 喻 ("metaphor")

Yu Yan 俞琰

Yuanshi 元始 (Original Commencement)

Yuanyang zi 元陽子

Yuanyou 遠遊 (Far Roaming)

Yunji qiqian 雲笈七籤 (Seven Lots
from the Bookbag of the Clouds)

zaohua 造化 ("creation")

zhan 戰 ("to fight")

zhang 丈 (a unit of length)

Zhang Boduan 張伯端

Zhang Daoling 張道陵

Zhao Yizhen 趙宜真

zhen geng 震庚

Zheng Xuan 鄭玄

zhentu 真土 (True Soil)

zhenyou 真有 ("true existence")

zhi 志 (will)

zhi 治 ("to control")

zhi 知 (knowledge)

Zhigui ji 指歸集 (Anthology Pointing
to Where One Belongs)

Zhixuan pian 指玄篇 (Pointing to the
Mystery)

Zhong Lü chuandao ji 鍾呂傳道集
(Records of the Transmission of
the Dao from Zhongli Quan to Lü
Dongbin)

zhonghe 中和 ("median harmony")

Zhongli Quan 鍾離權

Zhouyi lüeli 周易略例 (General Introduction to the Book of Changes)

zhu 主 ("master," "host")

zhu 銖 (a unit of weight)

Zhuangzi 莊子 (Book of Master
Zhuang)

zhusha 朱砂 (Red Cinnabar)

zi 子 (one of the twelve earthly
branches)

Zuozhuan 左傳 (Zuo's Commentary
[to the *Springs and Autumns*])

Works Quoted

Sources

Texts in the Taoist Canon (*Daozang* 道藏) are numbered according to Kristofer Schipper, *Concordance du Tao-tsang: Titres des ouvrages* (Paris: École Française d'Extrême-Orient, 1975), abbreviated as "CT."

Bichuan Zhengyang zhenren Lingbao bifa 祕傳正陽真人靈寶畢法 [Secret Transmission of the True Man Zhengyang's Complete Methods of the Numinous Treasure]. Tenth century. Daozang, CT 1191.

Chen xiansheng neidan jue 陳先生內丹訣 [Instructions on the Internal Elixir by Master Chen]. Attributed to Chen Pu 陳朴, ca. tenth century. Daozang, CT 1096.

Chongyang zhenren jinguan yusuo jue 重陽真人金關玉鎖訣 [Instructions on the Golden Barrier and the Jade Lock by the True Man Wang Chongyang]. Attributed to Wang Zhe 王嚞 (1113–70). Daozang, CT 1156.

Cui gong ruyao jing zhujie 崔公入藥鏡注解 [Commentary and Explications on the *Mirror for Compounding the Medicine* by Master Cui]. Wang Jie 王玠 (?–ca. 1380). Daozang, CT 135.

Dadan zhizhi 大丹直指 [Straightforward Directions on the Great Elixir]. Attributed to Qiu Chuji 丘處機 (1148–1227). Daozang, CT 244.

Danfang xuzhi 丹房須知 [Required Knowledge for the Chamber of the Elixirs]. Wu Wu 吳悟, 1163. Daozang, CT 900.

Daode zhenjing jiyi 道德真經集義 [Collected Explanations on the *Daode jing*]. Liu Weiyong 劉惟永 et al., 1299. Daozang, CT 724.

Daofa huiyuan 道法會元 [Collected Essentials of Taoist Methods]. Early fifteenth century. Daozang, CT 1220.

Dengzhen yinjue 登真隱訣 [Concealed Instructions for the Ascent to Reality]. Tao Hongjing 陶弘景 (456–536). Daozang, CT 421.

Dongzhen Shangqing shenzhou qizhuan qibian wutian jing 洞真上清神州七轉七變舞天經 [Scripture of the Divine Continent on the Dance in Heaven in Seven Revolutions and Seven Transformations]. Orig. late fourth century. Daozang, CT 1331.

Falin biezhuan 法琳別傳 [Separate biography of Falin]. Yanzong 彥琮, second half of the seventh century. Taishō shinshu daizōkyō 大正新修大藏經, no. 2051.

Guang hongming ji 廣弘明集 [Expanded Collection Spreading the Light of Buddhism]. Daoxuan 道宣 (596–667). Taishō shinshu daizōkyō 大正新修大藏經, no. 2103.

Guwen longhu jing zhushu 古文龍虎經注疏 [Commentary and Sub-Commentary to the Ancient Text of the Scripture of the Dragon and Tiger]. Wang Dao 王道, 1185. Daozang, CT 996.

Haiqiong Bai zhenren yulu 海瓊白真人語錄 [Recorded Sayings of the True Man Bai Yuchan of Haiqiong]. Bai Yuchan 白玉蟾 (1194–1229?), ed. by Peng Si 彭耜, 1251. Daozang, CT 1307.

Huangdi yinfu jing jiasong jiezhu 黃帝陰符經夾頌解注 [Explications and Commentary on the *Scripture of the Hidden Response*, with Hymns]. Wang Jie 王玠 (?–ca. 1380). Daozang, CT 126.

Huangdi yinfu jing zhujie 黃帝陰符經注解 [Commentary and Explications on the *Scripture of the Hidden Response*]. Ren Zhaoyi 任照一, Northern Song. Daozang, CT 114.

Huangqi yangjing jing 黃氣陽精經 [Scripture of the Yellow Breath and the Yang Essence]. Orig. late fourth century. Daozang, CT 33.

Huanjin shu 還金述 [On the Return to Gold]. Tao Zhi 陶植, ca. 800. Daozang, CT 922.

Huanzhen ji 還真集 [Anthology of Reverting to Reality]. Wang Jie 王玠 (?–ca. 1380). Daozang, CT 1074.

Huizhen ji 會真集 [Anthology of Gathering Authenticity]. Wang Jichang 王吉昌 (fl. 1220–40). Daozang, CT 247.

Hunyuan bajing zhenjing 混元八景真經 [True Scripture of the Eight Luminous Spirits of the Inchoate Origin]. Early twelfth century? Daozang, CT 660.

Jindan fu 金丹賦 [Rhapsody on the Golden Elixir]. Tao Zhi 陶植 (ca. 800), commentary by Ma Lizhao 馬蒞昭 (Yuan dynasty). Daozang, CT 261.

Jindan sibai zi 金丹四百字 [Four Hundred Words on the Golden Elixir]. Attributed to Zhang Boduan 張伯端 (ca. 987–1082); commentary by Huang Ziru 黃自如 (fl. 1241). Daozang, CT 1081.

Jindan zhengzong 金丹正宗 [Correct Lineage of the Golden Elixir]. Hu Huncheng 胡混成, Song dynasty. Daozang, CT 1087.

Jindan zhizhi 金丹直指 [Straightforward Directions on the Golden Elixir]. 1250. Daozang, CT 1072.

Jinye huandan yinzheng tu 金液還丹印證圖 [Charts for the Verification of the Golden Liquor and Cyclical Elixir]. Longmei zi 龍眉子, ca. 1222. Daozang, CT 151.

Longhu huandan jue 龍虎還丹訣 [Instructions on the Reverted Elixir of the Dragon and Tiger]. Commentary by Li zhenren 李真人, Northern Song. Daozang, CT 1084.

Longhu huandan juesong 龍虎還丹訣頌 [Ode on the Instructions on the Reverted Elixir of the Dragon and Tiger]. Lin Taigu 林太古, commentary by Gushen zi 谷神子, Northern Song. Tenth century. Daozang, CT 1082.

Mei xian guanji 梅仙觀記 [Records of the Abbey of the Immortal Mei Fu]. Ca. 1296. Daozang, CT 600.

Qing'an Yingchan zi yulu 清庵瑩蟾子語錄 [Recorded Sayings of (Li) Qing'an, Master of the Shining Toad]. Li Daochun 李道純 (fl. ca. 1290); ed. by Cai Zhiyi 蔡志頤 et al. Ca. 1300. Daozang, CT 1060.

Quanzhen jixuan biyao 全真集玄祕要 [Collected Mysteries and Secret Essentials of Quanzhen]. Li Daochun 李道純 (fl. ca. 1290). Daozang, CT 251.

Sandong zhunang 三洞珠囊 [Pearl Satchel of the Three Caverns]. Wang Xuanhe 王懸和, late seventh century. Daozang, CT 1139.

Sanji zhiming quanti 三極至命筌蹄 [Guidance on the Three Ultimates and the Supreme Destiny]. Wang Qingsheng 王慶升, thirteenth century. Daozang, CT 275.

Shangdong xindan jingjue 上洞心丹經訣 [Instructions on the Scripture of the Heart Elixir of the Highest Cavern]. Tang dynasty. Daozang, CT 950.

Shangqing Lingbao dafa 上清靈寶大法 [Great Rites of the Numinous Treasure of Highest Clarity]. Wang Qizhen's 王契真 (fl. ca. 1250). Daozang, CT 1221.

Shangqing waiguo fangpin Qingtong neiwen 上清外國放品青童內文 [Inner Script of the Azure Lad on the Distribution of the Outer Realms]. Orig. late fourth century. Daozang, CT 1373.

Shangqing yuanshi bianhua baozhen shangjing jiuling taimiao Guishan xuanlu 上清元始變化寶真上經九靈太妙龜山玄籙 [Mysterious Register of the Turtle Mountain from the Great Wonder of (the Palace of) the Nine Numina, Pertaining to the True and Superior Scripture of Highest Clarity on the Transformations of the Original Beginning]. Orig. late fourth century. Daozang, CT 1393.

Shangsheng xiuzhen sanyao 上乘修真三要 [The Three Principles of the Cultivation of Reality According to the Highest Vehicle]. Gao Daokuan 高道寬 (1195–1277). Daozang, CT 267.

Shangyang zi jindan dayao 上陽子金丹大要 [Great Essentials of the Golden Elixir]. Chen Zhixu 陳致虛 (1290–ca. 1368). Daozang, CT 1067.

Shangyang zi jindan dayao tu 上陽子金丹大要圖 [Great Essentials of the Golden Elixir: Charts]. Chen Zhixu 陳致虛 (1290–ca. 1368). Daozang, CT 1068.

Sun zhenren beiji qianjin yaofang 孫真人備急十金要方 [Essential Prescriptions Worth a Thousand, for Urgent Need, by the True Man Sun Simiao]. Sun Simiao 孫思邈, seventh century. Daozang, CT 1163.

Taigu ji 太古集 [Anthology of Master Taigu]. Hao Datong 郝大通 (1140–1213). Daozang, CT 1161.

Taishang Dongxuan Lingbao Tianzun shuo Luotian dajiao shangpin miaojing 太上洞玄靈寶天尊説羅天大醮上品妙經 [Wondrous Superior Scripture of the Great Offering of All Heaven Spoken by the Celestial Worthy of the Numinous Treasure]. Southern Song dynasty. Daozang, CT 1194.

Taishang huadao dushi xianjing 太上化道度世仙經 [Scripture of the Immortals of the Most High on the Transformation into the Dao and the Salvation of the World]. Song dynasty? Daozang, CT 648.

Taishang jiuyao xinyin miaojing 太上九要心印妙經 [Most High Wondrous Scripture of the Mind Seal and Its Nine Essentials]. Song dynasty? Daozang, CT 225.

Taishang Laojun shuo wudou jinzhang shousheng jing 太上老君説五斗金章受生經 [Scripture of the Golden Emblems of the Five Dippers Conferring Life, Spoken by the Most High Lord Lao]. Song dynasty? Daozang, CT 653.

Taishang Lingbao tiandi yundu ziran miaojing 太上靈寶天地運度自然妙經 [Scripture of the Most High Numinous Treasure on the Laws of Movement of Heaven and Earth]. Sixth century. Daozang, CT 322.

Taishang miaoshi jing 太上妙始經 [Most High Scripture of the Wondrous Beginning]. Fifth century? Daozang, CT 658.

Taizhen Yudi siji mingke jing 太真玉帝四極明科經 [Great and True Scripture of the Illustrious Code of the Four Poles of the Jade Emperor]. Six Dynasties. Daozang, CT 184.

Xianquan ji 峴泉集 [Anthology of Mountain Springs]. Zhang Yuchu 張宇初 (1361–1410). Daozang, CT 1311.

Xiantian xuanmiao yunü taishang shengmu zichuan xiandao 先天玄妙玉女太上聖母資傳仙道 [The Way of Immortality Transmitted by the Most High Holy Mother, Precelestial Jade Woman of Obscure Mystery]. Tang dynasty. Daozang, CT 868.

Xishan qunxian huizhen ji 西山群仙會真記 [Records of the Gathered Immortals and Assembled True Men of the Western Hills]. Attributed to Shi Jianwu 施肩吾 (fl. 820–35). Daozang, CT 246.

Xiudan miaoyong zhili lun 修丹妙用至理論 [Treatise on the Ultimate Principles of the Wondrous Operation of the Cultivation of the Elixir]. Northern Song dynasty. Daozang, CT 234.

Xiuzhen shishu 修真十書 [Ten Books on the Cultivation of Reality]. Late thirteenth or early fourteenth century. Daozang, CT 263.

Xuanzong zhizhi wanfa tonggui 玄宗直指萬法同歸 [Reintegrating the Ten Thousand Dharmas: A Straightforward Explanation of the Taoist Tradition]. Mu Changzhao 牧常晁, twelfth century. Daozang, CT 1066.

Yuanyang zi fayu 原陽子法語 [Exemplary Sayings of the Master of Primary Yang]. Zhao Yizhen 趙宜真, late fourteenth century. Daozang, CT 1071.

Yuanyang zi jinye ji 元陽子金液集 [The Golden Liquor, a Collection by the Master of Original Yang]. Ninth century. Daozang, CT 238.

Wenchang dadong xianjing 玉清無極總真文昌大洞仙經 [Scripture of Immortality of the Great Cavern according to Wenchang]. Commentary by Wei Qi 衛琪, 1309. Daozang, CT 103.

Zhigui ji 指歸集 [Anthology Pointing to Where One Belongs]. Wu Wu 吳悟, 1165. Daozang, CT 921.

Zhonghe ji 中和集 [Anthology of Central Harmony]. Li Daochun 李道純 (fl. ca. 1290). Daozang, CT 249.

Zhouyi cantong qi 周易參同契 [Token for Joining the Three in Accordance with the Book of Changes]. Ca. 700. Daozang, CT 999.

Zhouyi cantong qi fahui 周易參同契發揮 [Explanation of the *Token for Joining the Three in Accordance with the Book of Changes*]. Yu Yan 俞琰 (1258–1314), 1284. Daozang, CT 1005.

Zhouyi cantong qi fenzhang tong zhenyi 周易參同契分章通真義 [True Meaning of the *Token for Joining the Three in Accordance with the Book of Changes*, with a Subdivision into Sections]. Peng Xiao 彭曉 (?–955), 947. Daozang, CT 1002.

Zhouyi cantong qi zhu 周易參同契注 [Commentary to the *Token for Joining the Three in Accordance with the Book of Changes*]. Prob. thirteenth century. Daozang, CT 1000.

Zhouyi tu 周易圖 [Charts of the *Book of Changes*]. Yuan dynasty? Daozang, CT 157.

Ziyang zhenren wuzhen pian jiangyi 紫陽真人悟真篇講義 [Explaining the Meaning of *Awakening to Reality* by the True Man of Purple Yang]. Xia Yuanding 夏元鼎 (fl. 1225–27). Daozang, CT 146.

Ziyang zhenren wuzhen pian sanzhu 紫陽真人悟真篇三注 [Three Commentaries to *Awakening to Reality* by the True Man of Purple Yang]. Commentaries by Xue Daoguang 薛道光 (?–1191, actually written by Weng Baoguang 翁葆光, fl. 1173), Lu Ziye 陸子野 (thirteenth century?), and Chen Zhixu 陳致虛 (1290–ca. 1368), edited by Zhang Shihong 張士弘 (fourteenth century). Daozang, CT 142.

Ziyang zhenren wuzhen pian zhushu 紫陽真人悟真篇注疏 [Commentary and Subcommentary to *Awakening to Reality* by the True Man of Purple Yang]. Weng Baoguang 翁葆光 (preface dated 1173), ed. by Dai Qizong 戴起宗 (preface dated 1335). Daozang, CT 141.

Ziyang zhenren wuzhen zhizhi xiangshuo sansheng biyao 紫陽真人悟真直指
詳説三乘祕要 [Straightforward Directions and Detailed Explanations on
Awakening to Reality and the Secret Essentials of the Three Vehicles].
Weng Baoguang 翁葆光, 1337. Daozang, CT 143.

Studies

Baldrian-Hussein, Farzeen. "Inner Alchemy: Notes on the Origin and Use of
the Term *Neidan*." *Cahiers d'Extrême-Asie* 5 (1989–90): 163–90.

————. *Procédés Secrets du Joyau Magique: Traité d'alchimie taoïste du XIe
siècle*. Paris: Les Deux Océans, 1984.

Billeter, Jean-François. *L'art chinois de l'écriture*. Genève: Skira-Flammarion,
1989.

Bouveresse, Jacques. *Le mythe de l'intériorité: Expérience, signification et
langage privé chez Wittgenstein*. Paris: Éditions de Minuit, 1987.

Chen Guofu 陳國符. *Daozang yuanliu kao* 道藏源流考 [Studies on the
origins and development of the Taoist Canon]. 2 vols. Beijing: Zhonghua
shuju, 1963.

Couvreur, Séraphin. *La chronique de la Principauté de Lou*. 3 vols. Tien-tsin:
Cathasia, 1951.

Granet, Marcel. *La pensée chinoise*. Paris: La Renaissance du Livre, 1934.

Greimas, Algirdas Julien. *Du sens*. Vol. 2: *Essais sémiotiques*. Paris: Éditions
du Seuil, 1983.

Hall, David L., and Roger T. Ames. *Thinking Through Confucius*. Albany:
State University of New York Press, 1987.

Ho, Ping-yü, and Joseph Needham. "The Laboratory Equipment of the Early
Medieval Chinese Alchemist." *Ambix* 7 (1959): 57–116.

Jullien, F. *Procès ou création: Une introduction à la pensée des lettrés chinois*.
Paris: Éditions du Seuil, 1989.

Kalinowski Marc. *Cosmologie et divination dans la Chine ancienne: Le
Compendium des Cinq Agents (Wuxing dayi, VIe siècle)*. Paris: École
Française d'Extrême-Orient, 1991.

————. "La transmission du dispositif des Neuf Palais sous les Six-
Dynasties." In Michel Strickmann, ed., *Tantric and Taoist Studies in
Honour of Rolf A. Stein*, III:773–811. Bruxelles: Institut Belge des Hautes
Études Chinoises, 1985.

Lagerwey John. *Taoist Ritual in Chinese Society and History*. New York:
Macmillan, 1987.

Li Yuanguo 李远国. *Daojiao qigong yangshengxue* 道教气功养生学 [Taoist *qigong* and the Nourishment of Life]. Chengdu: Sichuan sheng Shehui Kexueyuan chubanshe, 1988.

Needham, Joseph. *Science and Civilisation in China*, vol. V: *Chemistry and Chemical Technology*, part 5: *Spagyrical Discovery and Invention: Physiological Alchemy*. With the collaboration of Lu Gwei-Djen. Cambridge: Cambridge University Press, 1983.

Robinet, Isabelle. *Introduction à l'alchimie intérieure taoïste: De l'unité et de la multiplicité*. Paris: Le Cerf, 1994.

———. *La révélation du Shangqing dans l'histoire du taoïsme*. 2 vols. Paris: École Française d'Extrême-Orient, 1984.

———. *Les commentaires du Tao tö king jusqu'au VIIe siècle*. Paris: Collège de France, Institut des Hautes Études Chinoises, 1977.

———. "The Place and Meaning of the Notion of *Taiji* in Taoist Sources prior to the Ming Dynasty." *History of Religions* 29 (1990): 373–411.

Schipper, Kristofer M., and Wang Hsiu-huei. 1986. "Progressive and Regressive Time Cycles in Taoist Ritual." In J.T. Fraser, N. Lawrence, and F.C. Haber, eds., *Time, Science, and Society in China and the West*, 185–205. Amherst: University of Massachusetts Press, 1986.

Seidel, Anna. *La divination de Lao tseu dans le Taoïsme des Han*. Paris: École Française d'Extrême-Orient, 1969.

Sivin, Nathan. "The Theoretical Background of Elixir Alchemy." In Joseph Needham, *Science and Civilisation in China*, vol. V: *Chemistry and Chemical Technology*, part 4: *Spagyrical Discovery and Invention: Apparatus, Theories and Gifts*, 210–305. Cambridge: Cambridge University Press.

Solomon, Bernard. "'One is no Number' in China and the West." *Harvard Journal of Asiatic Studies* 17 (1954): 253–60.

Strickmann, Michel. "On the Alchemy of T'ao Hung-ching." In Holmes Welch and Anna Seidel, eds., *Facets of Taoism: Essays in Chinese Religion*, 123–92. New Haven and London: Yale University Press.

Vandermeersch, Léon. *Wangdao ou la voie royale*. 2 vols. Paris: Publications de l'EFEO, 1980.

Watson, Burton. *The Complete Works of Chuang Tzu*. New York: Columbia University Press, 1968.

Zürcher, Erik. "Buddhist Influence on Early Taoism: A Survey of Scriptural Evidence." *T'oung Pao* 66 (1980): 84–147.

Golden Elixir Press

www.goldenelixir.com
info@goldenelixir.com

Golden Elixir Press publishes dependable and affordable books
on Taoism, Taoist alchemy, and other traditional doctrines,
in print and as e-books

Fabrizio Pregadio, *The Seal of the Unity of the Three: A Study and Translation of the* Cantong qi, *the Source of the Taoist Way of the Golden Elixir.* Forthcoming.

Isabelle Robinet, *The World Upside Down: Essays on Taoist Internal Alchemy.* 2011.

Wang Mu, *Foundations of the Internal Elixir: The Taoist Practice of Neidan.* 2011.

Ananda K. Coomaraswamy, *Hinduism and Buddhism.* 2011.

Jami, *Flashes of Light: A Treatise on Sufism.* 2010.

Shaikh Sharfuddin Maneri, *Letters from a Sufi Teacher.* 2010.

Fabrizio Pregadio, *Awakening to Reality: The "Regulated Verses" of the* Wuzhen pian, *a Taoist Classic of Internal Alchemy.* 2009.

Fabrizio Pregadio, *Chinese Alchemy: An Annotated Bibliography of Works in Western Languages.* 2009.

Fabrizio Pregadio, *Index of Zhonghua Daozang.* 2009.

Made in the USA
San Bernardino, CA
01 October 2013